With *Art* in Mind

A Collection of Sixty Art Lessons Patricia Parker Groebner

 Bob Jones University Press
Greenville, South Carolina 29614

Library of Congress Cataloging-in-Publication Data

Groebner, Patricia Parker, 1935-
      With art in mind : a collection of sixty art lessons / Patricia
Parker Groebner.
            p.   cm.
      ISBN 1-57924-305-3
      1. Art—Study and teaching (Elementary)—United States.
I. Title.
      N362.G76 2000
      372.5'2044—dc21   99-41052
                                                                    CIP

Photograph Credits

Corel Corporation: Cover, 1, 23, 55, 115, 127, 157, 185 (backgrounds)
Creation Science Foundation, Ltd., Australia: 106
PhotoDisc, Inc.: Cover, i, 55, 127, 185 (insets)
Unusual Films: Cover, i, 1, 23, 115, 157 (insets)

NOTE: The fact that materials produced by other publishers may be referred to in this volume does not constitute an endorsement by Bob Jones University Press of the content or theological position of materials produced by such publishers. The position of Bob Jones University Press, and of the University itself, is well known. Any references and ancillary materials are listed as an aid to the reader and in an attempt to maintain the accepted academic standards of the publishing industry.

With Art in Mind: A Collection of Sixty Art Lessons

Coordinating author: Mary Ann Lumm

Editors: Elizabeth B. Berg and V. Edward Myers

Designers: Holly Gilbert and Brian Johnson

Compositor: Kelley Moore

© 2000 Bob Jones University Press
Greenville, South Carolina 29614

Printed in the United States of America

ISBN 1-57924-305-3

15 14 13 12 11 10 9 8 7 6 5 4 3 2

CONTENTS

CONTENTS

CONTENTS

INTRODUCTION

These sixty art lessons represent the most enjoyable and successful lessons that the author, Patricia Parker Groebner, used during her thirty-three years of teaching art to children. Each lesson is based on important art elements and principles, and each helps the students develop basic skills that are useful in all areas of life and learning.

Since art training and resources are frequently limited, all of these lessons are based on simple, step-by-step procedures that can be followed easily by persons with little or no formal art background. The lessons use materials that can be obtained inexpensively and stored easily. They are appropriate for students ages eight through thirteen, with a color key indicating whether the lesson is best for younger (blue), intermediate (red), or older (yellow) students within that range. Many of the lessons can be used with even younger or older students. Their flexibility allows them to be used in any sequence or with a group of students of mixed ages. Older students will generally produce a more complex and skillfully accomplished result, but all can benefit from the thinking, learning, and doing processes involved.

God created and placed mankind in a world of beauty, and His Word instructs us to "Let all things be done decently and in order" (I Cor. 14:40). Art in the broad sense is bringing order and beauty out of chaos. These lessons and their accompanying examples will aid you as you help your students enjoy art and learn from it. Pages viii-xiv provide helpful information and tips from Ms. Groebner and coordinating author Mary Ann Lumm on the teaching of art and the structure and goals of these lessons. You will profit from taking a few minutes to read those pages before beginning work on the lessons.

WHY TEACH ART?

- To encourage the students to observe and appreciate the order and beauty in creation and to praise God for it
- To strengthen the students' perception, contemplation, and ability to see beneath surface appearances
- To develop the students' knowledge and understanding of themselves, other people, and the world around them
- To encourage the students to develop and use whatever abilities God has given them to bring order and beauty into their work and their surroundings
- To present problems with many possible solutions, thus helping the students learn to be flexible and confident in working through uncertainties
- To help the students learn to set goals for themselves and to discipline themselves to achieve those goals
- To help the students learn to enjoy decision making, selecting, putting in order, and arranging—thus encouraging orderly thought processes and orderly work
- To help the students learn to use their physical, mental, and emotional capabilities together
- To help the students develop imaginative and individual thinking (necessary for planning and initiative) along with responsibility and the ability to make sound judgments
- To provide experience with a variety of media while mastering different skills
- To provide a way for the students to express their thoughts and feelings in a productive, visual manner
- To develop the students' knowledge and understanding of the art of other nations, cultures, and times

THE LESSONS

- Lessons are grouped into units according to media. A more complete list of suggested materials is given at the beginning of each lesson.

- Concepts and skills used in the lesson are noted in the sidebar. These notations are not intended to be exhaustive or limiting.

- Directions for lessons have been kept as brief and uncomplicated as possible; the samples show more of what is expected and possible results.

- To avoid potential problems and to provide an additional teaching sample, try each lesson yourself before you teach it.

- The time for each lesson will vary depending upon the complexity of the lesson and the abilities of the students.

- Most of the samples in this book have been reduced for reproduction, usually from 9" $\times$ 12", 12" $\times$ 18", or 18" $\times$ 24".

- When the directions instruct the students to sketch a picture, any subject matter could be used for the lesson, depending upon your directives, student interest, current study topics, and so forth. However, the students should be given more motivation than this brief instruction before they begin work (see Motivation Tips on the next page).

MOTIVATION TIPS

- Whenever possible, let the students know why they are doing what they are doing.

- Use field trips, stories, poems, songs, films, videos, recordings, photographs, unusual objects, pets, books with many photographs, and so forth to stimulate ideas and interest.

- Use questions and discussions to develop interest and to expand ideas. If a student is having difficulty coming up with a subject, avoid telling him to "just draw anything." Suggest several possible ideas and attempt to stimulate the student's thinking.

- Provide experiences with a variety of media and processes.

- Use a demonstration if processes are somewhat technical or students are not familiar with the possibilities of the materials.

- Show examples when first explaining the lesson, but do not display these as patterns for the students to copy.

- Organize the lesson preparation so that the students can begin work as soon as they are adequately instructed and motivated.

- Frame (or mount) and display finished work to enhance the art and to give it the importance it deserves, thus motivating the students for future lessons. Frames need not be elaborate; reusable paper ones are fine as long as they are neatly made.

MATERIALS TIPS

- Use only materials you would want to use yourself for high-quality artwork. Materials that are inadequate, inappropriate, or of poor quality can be very frustrating for students to use and can significantly affect the quality of their work.

- Provide large, easily handled materials for younger students.

- The materials listed in each lesson are suggestions that produce the results shown in the samples. However, availability and your own preferences may affect which materials you use. Changing materials can sometimes change the look of the entire lesson—an exciting, flexible, and desirable aspect of these lessons.

- Develop a regular system for handing out and collecting materials, having the students help as much as possible.

- Arrange the work area for efficiency and for quick, simple clean-up.

- Use newspapers as "cushions" for making crayon work easier, brighter, and waxier; they also protect work areas when using glue, paint, chalk, and so forth.

- Provide each student with a damp paper towel for wiping fingers while working with chalks or paint.

- Have the students wear old shirts or smocks to protect their clothing when using messy materials.

- For watercolor or tempera painting, use paper that will not disintegrate or curl easily. Large sheets of 80 lb. white drawing paper work well. Paper specifically made for watercolor is even better but more expensive; you might consider it for older, more advanced students.

- Add a few drops of liquid detergent to tempera paint or drawing ink to make paint more pliable, add elasticity, reduce chipping of thickly applied paint, and make ink or paint more "washable."

- Distribute tempera paint on paper plates or frozen dinner trays. Each student should have two plates—one for his paint supply and one for mixing colors. Give each student a small amount of each paint color initially and more as needed.

- Inexpensive hair spray in an aerosol can works well as fixative to help protect chalk work from smearing.

- Properly clean and store all materials as soon as possible after use. Brushes should never be left resting on their bristles, either in a water container during the lesson or when stored; always place them flat or with bristles up.

- Allow ample time for clean-up procedures. Teach the students to be responsible for cleaning up their own work areas.

- Teach the students to work safely. Handle materials and tools carefully and respectfully, and be alert to any safety notes in the lessons or on material labels.

METHODS TIPS

- Establish a pleasant and enjoyable atmosphere for art, but do not treat the art lesson as "playtime."

- Encourage thinking and initiative rather than imitation.

- Once the student has begun, observe him to be sure he understands what he is doing. Use the lesson time to encourage, to help as needed, and to be alert to what he is trying to express and accomplish. Encourage him to tell you about his work. Compliment him on attractive use of line, color, shape, pattern, or other aspects of his work.

- If the student is "stuck," discuss ideas with him to help him get his thoughts clarified. If he is dissatisfied with his work, resist showing him "how to do it right" (other than demonstrating technical processes); try to expand his knowledge and motivation so he can do his own work.

- Encourage the students to be aware of characteristic qualities of materials.

- Allow for individual differences in working speed. Give enough time so that the slow students will not be rushed into doing careless work. Be prepared with extra work for the speedy students, but try first to encourage further thinking and enhancement of their original work (particularly if little effort has been put into it).

- If your background and resources allow, provide historical background for an art lesson or show reproductions or original works of art. Especially with older students, discuss the art principles (rhythm, balance, unity, variety, emphasis, and proportion) that can be found in these works and in the students' work. Explain ways in which the art elements (line, shape, form, color, value, texture, and pattern) are used to achieve art principles (see Art Elements and Principles on page xiv).

- Teach respect for the work area, materials, tools, one's own work, and the work of others.

EVALUATION TIPS

- Remember that at this stage the art process and what it can do for the development of the students are more important than the art product.

- Remember that children represent things in their artwork as they understand and see them; their art expression will change and develop as their knowledge and perceptions develop.

- Consider whether each student's work shows honest individual effort and depicts ideas and things that he is interested in, knows about, and understands. Emotional, physical, and mental experience and symbolism will be represented; therefore, do not evaluate on the basis of how "realistic" or "lifelike" the picture appears to you.

- Consider whether each student's work is original, flexible, interesting, pleasing, well organized, and effective in conveying ideas.

- Consider how well each student understood and followed the instructions and how carefully and skillfully he handled his materials and tools.

- Praise the good qualities in the student's work and build his confidence whenever possible, but never praise haphazard or uncaring work. Do not allow the student to be satisfied with minimal efforts.

- Display work whenever space permits, particularly when the student has done work that reflects well his abilities and lesson requirements.

ART ELEMENTS AND PRINCIPLES

▶ ELEMENTS

- Line—path of a moving dot; can vary in width, direction, length, and character
- Shape (or space)—two-dimensional area set off by line, color, or value
- Form (or mass)—area that appears three-dimensional
- Color—visible light rays reflected by an area; has properties of hue (name), value (light or dark), intensity (purity), and temperature (warm or cool)
- Value—lightness or darkness
- Texture—how something feels, or appears that it would feel, to the touch
- Pattern—surface design or decoration made up of repeated lines, shapes, colors, or textures

▶ PRINCIPLES

- Rhythm—a sense of controlled movement produced by repetition or progressive change in design elements
- Balance—a sense of stability and equilibrium produced by equal distribution of visual weight or attraction
- Unity (or harmony)—visually pleasing feeling of oneness and belonging together
- Variety (or contrast)—change sufficient to prevent monotony and add interest
- Emphasis (or dominance)—accenting a part by size, shape, color, texture, lines, or position
- Proportion—relationship of parts to each other or to the whole work of art

BLACK MARKERS/ DRAWING INK

8 LESSONS ➤

BUBBLE AQUARIUMS

▶ Suggested Materials

- 12" × 12" white paper
- Round object (e.g., a plate, pie tin, or wastebasket) for each student to use to draw a large circle
- Pencils
- Sea-life pictures
- Scrap paper
- Scissors
- Compasses
- Black markers
- Rulers

▶ Directions

1. Draw a large circle (bubble) on 12" × 12" paper by tracing around the round object.

2. Draw one sea creature design on scrap paper; cut it out.

3. Trace around the sea creature several times inside the bubble, turning it various ways. When it overlaps the edge of the bubble, draw only the part inside.

4. Use a compass to draw circles (bubbles) of different sizes overlapping sea creatures and other circles (bubbles).

5. Trace over all lines with a black marker.
   Note: For younger students, omit steps 6-9 (see next page).

6. Use a pencil to lightly mark sections: B (black), W (white), and S (striped).

7. Make sure no section adjoins another section with the same letter (except possibly two white).

8. Fill in black and striped sections using a black marker. Erase the pencil mark labeling each section before filling that section. Erase the marks on the white sections when done.

9. Use rulers to make straight, evenly spaced, close-together stripes.

10. Cut out the large bubble for display.

Concepts: New shapes created by overlapping shapes and adding values; unity and rhythm through repetition and progressive transition; knowledge of shapes of sea creatures

Skills: Drawing; cutting; arranging; using rulers and markers

Steps 1-5

Black Markers/Drawing Ink

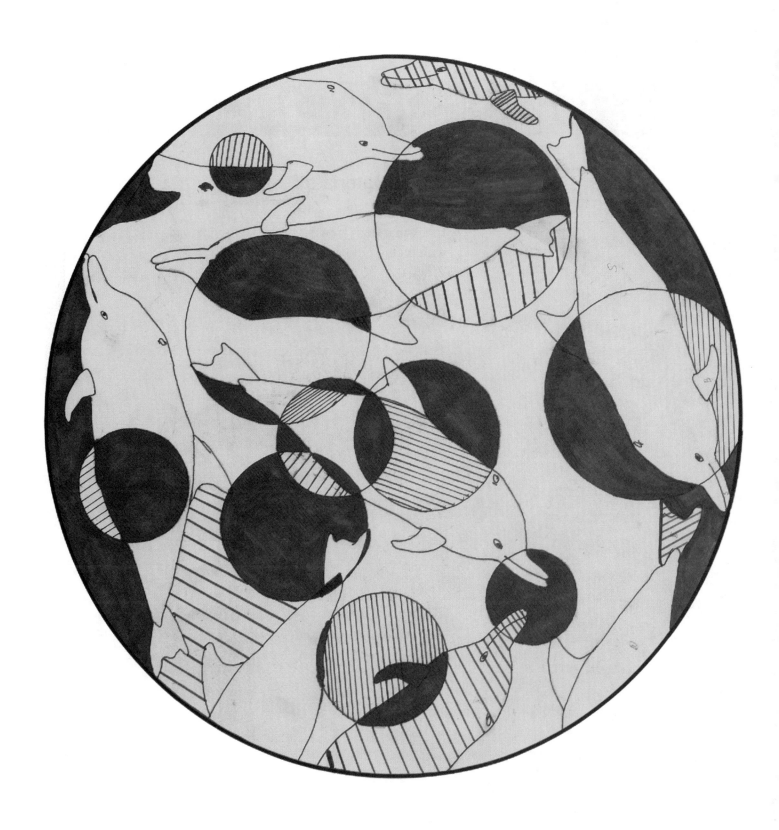

TEXTURES AND PATTERNS

▶ Suggested Materials

- 9" × 12" white paper
- Black markers (If available, drawing ink and pens could be used with older students.)
- Pencils

▶ Directions

1. Fold one sheet of paper into sixteen small sections.

2. With a black marker, use a variety of repeated or varied lines and shapes to create a different texture or pattern in each small section.

3. Sketch a picture with pencil on a second sheet of paper.

4. Trace over the pencil lines with marker or ink.

5. Fill open areas with a black marker, using some of your texture or pattern ideas from the first sheet.

Concepts: Using repeated or varied lines and shapes to create textures and patterns

Skills: Drawing; observing and producing visual textures and patterns

Black Markers/Drawing Ink

SCRIBBLE FIGURES

▶ Suggested Materials

- 12" × 18" white or colored paper
- Black markers

▶ Directions

1. Observe models (students in different poses).
2. With a black marker draw figures from the head down using circular scribble movements. Do not lift your marker from the paper.
3. Use scribble marks to give thickness to each figure.
4. Scatter many figures across your paper.

Concepts: Capturing proportions or actions quickly; using line to make a shape without outlining

Skills: Observing and drawing poses and actions

FLOATING BOXES

▶ **Suggested Materials**

- 12" × 18" white paper
- Pencils
- Rulers
- Black markers

▶ **Directions**

1. With a pencil draw nine rectangles (may include squares) of different sizes and shapes in three rows of three.

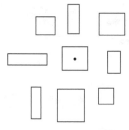

Concepts: Introduction to the term *vanishing point;* consistent use of shading

Skills: Using rulers; drawing; creating appearance of three dimensions and of linear perspective

2. Put a dot (vanishing point) in the center of the middle box.
3. Using a ruler, connect the upper right box with the vanishing point. Draw lines lightly to be able to erase easily.
4. Limit the size of the box to be outside the center box by drawing horizontal and vertical limits.

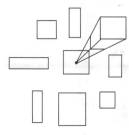

5. Erase lines no longer needed for the box (i.e., the lines between the vanishing point and the horizontal and vertical limits).
6. Shade the sides of the three-dimensional box.
7. Continue this procedure with all the boxes.
8. Trace over the edge lines of boxes with a black marker and ruler.

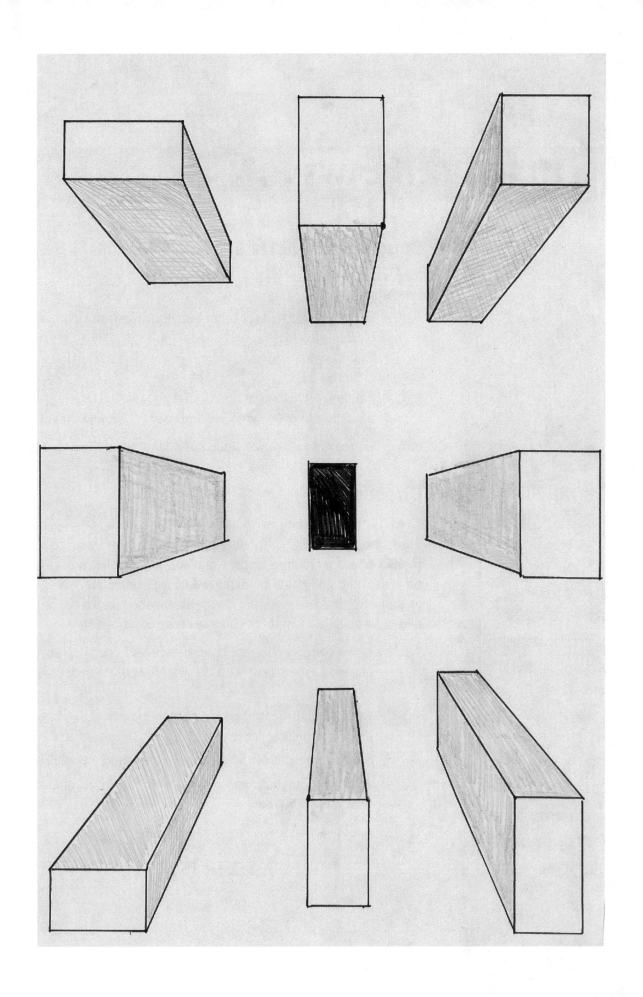

BLEACH DRAWING

▶ Suggested Materials

- Colored paper
- Bleach
- Baby food jar lids (or other small, difficult-to-tip containers) for bleach
- Cotton swabs
- Drawing ink
- Pointed 1/4" wooden dowel sticks
- Black markers (may be used instead of ink and dowel sticks)

Note: Test the colored paper since not all colors and brands bleach well.

▶ Directions

Note: Before beginning work, discuss what bleach is, how and when it is used, and the necessity of using it very carefully in order to avoid contact with eyes, skin, clothing, carpet, and so forth. If bleach accidentally gets on something that could be damaged, rinse immediately with lots of clear, clean water. If drawing ink is used, discuss the fact that it is permanent and must also be kept off clothing and surroundings.

1. Use a cotton swab dipped in bleach and one sheet of colored paper to experiment with the way the colored paper will react to the bleach.

2. On a second sheet of paper, draw a picture with a cotton swab dipped in bleach; let dry.

3. Sharpen the end of the dowel as you would a pencil.

4. Add detail, texture, and accents with the dowel dipped in ink or with a black marker.

Concepts: Removing (rather than adding) color; flexibility in choice and use of media and tools

Skills: Drawing with new media and tools with unusual qualities; perceiving and drawing light and dark surface areas rather than dark outlines

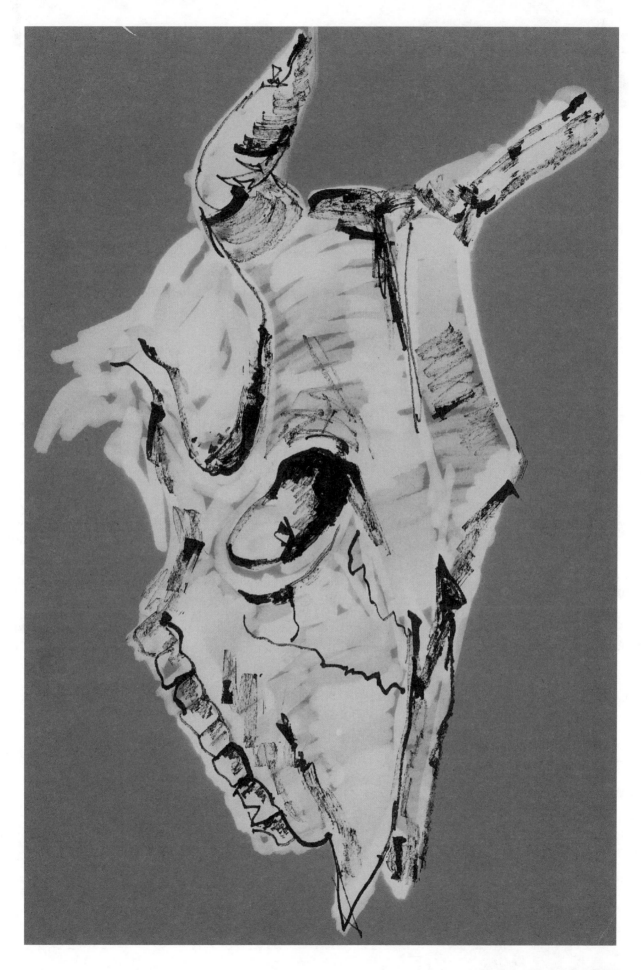

LESSON 6

BLEACH FIGURES

▶ **Suggested Materials**

- Colored paper
- Bleach
- Baby food jar lids (or other small, difficult-to-tip containers) for bleach
- Cotton swabs
- Drawing ink
- Pointed 1/4" wooden dowel sticks
- Black markers (may be used instead of ink and dowel sticks)

Note: Test the colored paper since not all colors and brands bleach well.

▶ **Directions**

Note: Before beginning work, discuss what bleach is, how and when it is used, and the necessity of using it very carefully in order to avoid contact with eyes, skin, clothing, carpet, and so forth. If bleach accidentally gets on something that could be damaged, rinse immediately with lots of clear, clean water. If drawing ink is used, discuss the fact that it is permanent and must also be kept off clothing and surroundings.

1. Use a cotton swab dipped in bleach and one sheet of colored paper to experiment with the way the colored paper will react to the bleach.
2. Observing a model, draw the figure on a second sheet of paper, using a cotton swab dipped in bleach; let dry.
3. Sharpen the end of the dowel as you would a pencil.
4. Draw and add details with the pointed dowel stick dipped in ink or with a black marker.

Concepts: Capturing proportions or actions quickly; removing color; flexibility in choice and use of media and tools

Skills: Drawing with new media and tools with unusual qualities; observing

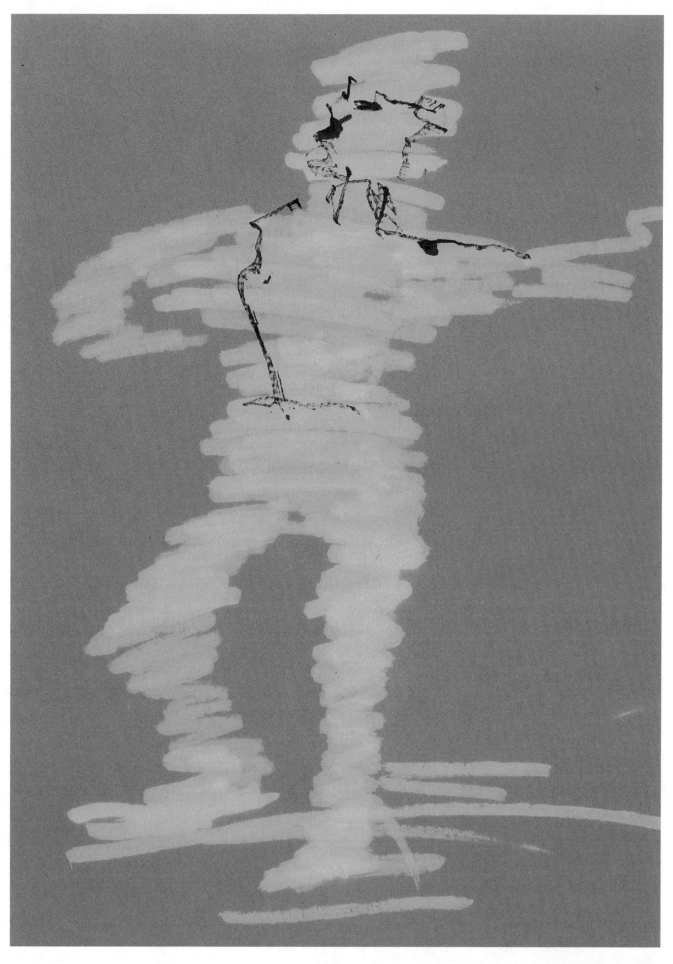

CRAYON ETCHING

▶ Suggested Materials

- 12" × 18" paper
- Pencils
- Crayons
- Drawing ink or black tempera
- Brushes (one-inch sponge brushes work well for this)
- Containers of water for cleaning brushes
- Paper clips (opened)

▶ Directions

Note: If using drawing ink, discuss the fact that it is permanent and must be handled with care to avoid getting on clothes or surroundings.

1. Draw a large picture in pencil on 12" × 18" paper.
2. Double ALL the outlines.
3. Do NOT color between the doubled lines forming the outline of objects and parts.
4. Color objects, parts, and background very heavily with bright, light colors of wax crayon.
5. Use a brush to completely cover paper with ink or tempera. Crayon areas will resist ink slightly and look different when dry. Space between doubled lines will become wide black outlines.
6. When thoroughly dry, use an opened paper clip to etch (scratch) textures in the ink covering crayon areas.

Concepts: Characteristics of wax crayon; removing and revealing color by etching; visual texture and unity through color and technique

Skills: Etching techniques; using crayons with ink or paint

LAYERED PAINTING

▶ Suggested Materials

- 12" × 18" paper
- Pencils
- Tempera paint
- Brushes (one-inch sponge brushes work well for this)
- Containers of water for cleaning brushes
- Drawing ink
- Container of water to rinse ink off painting
- Newspaper

▶ Directions

Note: Before beginning work, discuss the fact that drawing ink is permanent and must be handled with care to avoid getting on clothes or surroundings.

1. Draw a picture with a pencil. Keep the subject large and avoid tiny details.

2. Paint the picture and background with thick paint, using bright, light colors; leave pencil lines unpainted so black ink will not rinse away from them; allow to dry well.

3. Use a brush to completely cover paper with ink; allow to dry.

4. Immerse the paper in the water. Using a finger, rub the ink off sparingly. Be careful not to rub too hard and remove undercoat of bright colors as well.

5. Remove from the water and dry flat on newspaper.

Concepts: Removing and revealing color by rinsing; visual texture and unity through color and technique

Skills: Drawing; painting techniques using addition and subtraction of color

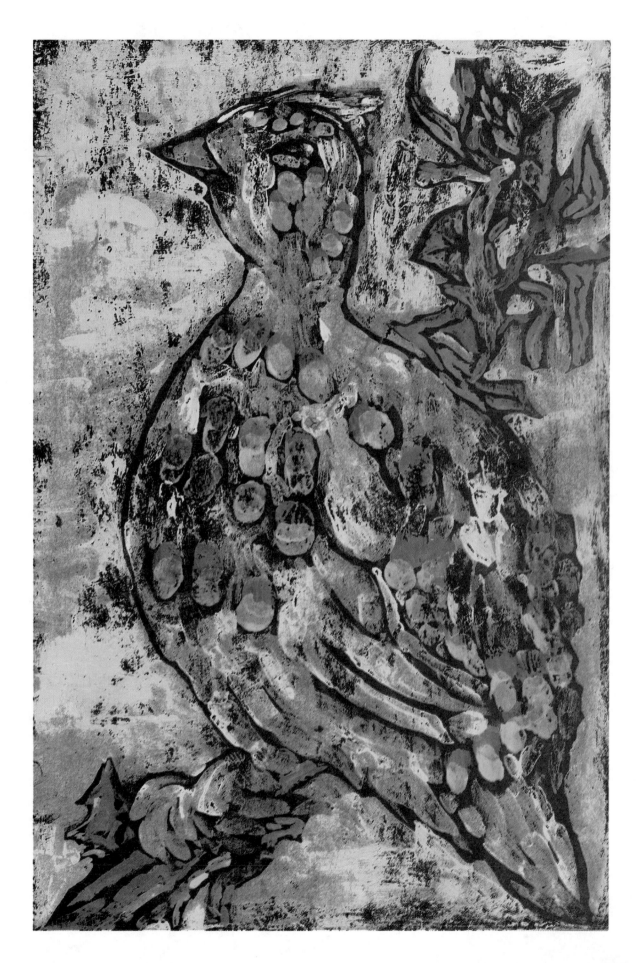

CHALKS/ PASTELS

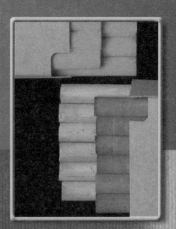

8 LESSONS ▶

CHALK MOIRE

▶ Suggested Materials

- 12" × 18" paper
- Scrap paper (at least 12" wide)
- Colored chalks or chalk pastels
- Tissues
- Fixative

▶ Directions

1. Tear an irregular edge along the 12" side of the scrap paper.
2. Apply chalk heavily to the torn edge of the strip.
3. Place the torn strip on top of a 12" × 18" piece of paper.
4. Use a tissue to rub chalk from the torn strip onto the background paper; use short, straight motions across the torn edge.
5. Move the torn strip and continue the rubbing procedure, filling the entire paper; add more chalk as necessary.
6. Another color of chalk may be used alternately.
7. Spray with fixative. Be sure to use only in a well-ventilated area.

Concepts: Soft textural qualities of chalk; filling the page; rhythm and unity through repetition and progressive transition

Skills: Tearing paper; using chalk

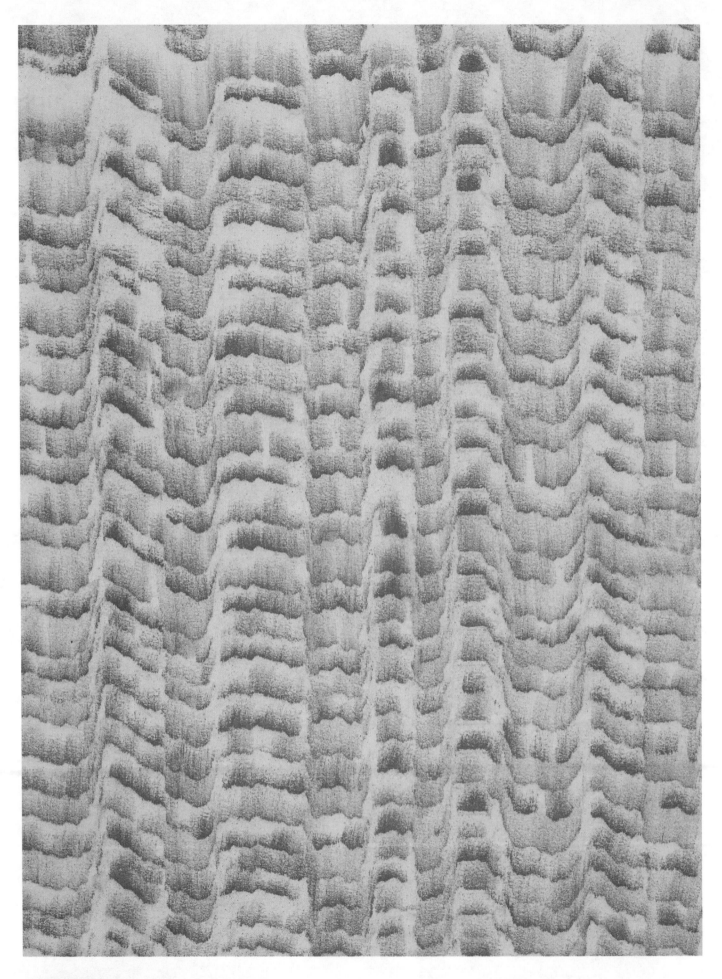

Chalks/Pastels

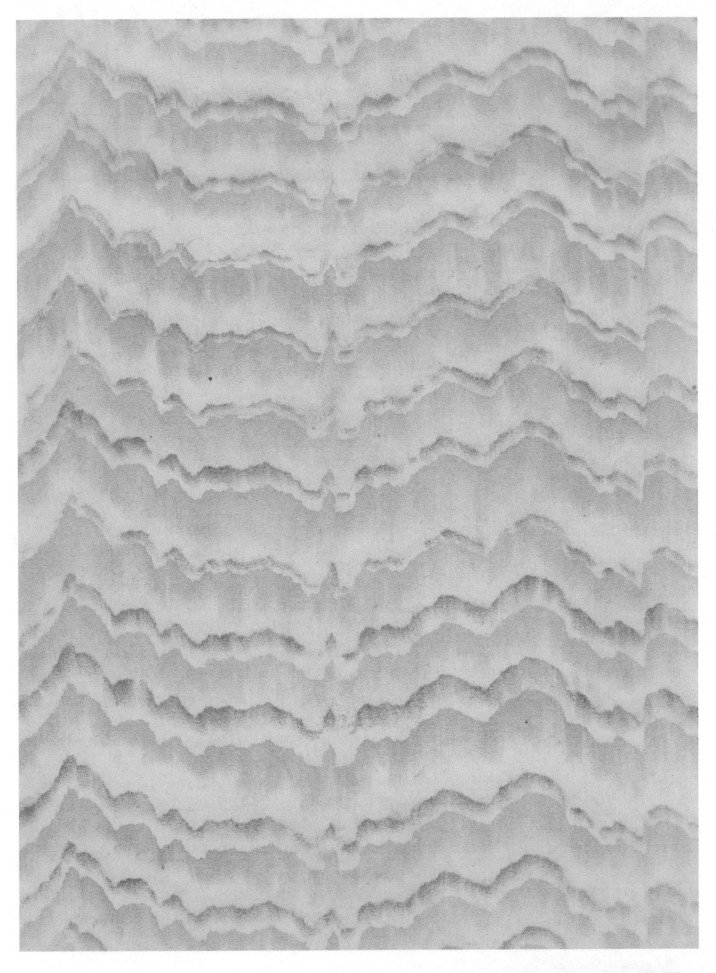

CHALK BLOSSOMS

► Suggested Materials

- 3" × 5" paper
- Scissors
- Colored chalks or chalk pastels
- 12" × 18" paper
- Tissues
- Fixative

► Directions

1. Fold 3" × 5" paper into fourths.
2. Cut a very tiny design at the center folded point.

3. Unfold the paper and apply chalk all around the hole.
4. Place the 3" × 5" paper onto a 12" × 18" paper (the background paper).
5. Use a tissue to rub chalk from the cut edge toward the center of the hole onto the background paper.
6. Scatter this design in several places on the paper. (Add more chalk as needed.)
7. Refold the 3" × 5" paper; make a second, different design cut around the first cut. (The second cut will eliminate the first cut, and the hole will be slightly larger.)
8. Repeat steps 3 through 5, placing the second design to surround the first.
9. Refold the paper; make a third and different cut.
10. Continue the procedure, making as many design cuts as possible—the more, the better!
11. Spray with fixative. Be sure to use only in a well-ventilated area.

Concepts: Soft textural qualities of chalk; filling the page; rhythm and unity through repetition and progressive transition

Skills: Cutting; arranging; using chalk; creating and using a stencil

Chalks/Pastels

STENCIL/FRISKET DESIGNS

▶ Suggested Materials

- Tagboard or thin, smooth cardboard (scrap manila folders work well)
- Scissors
- Colored chalks or chalk pastels
- 12" × 18" paper
- Tissues
- Fixative

▶ Directions

1. Cut an interesting variety of shapes from tagboard or cardboard. Make some shapes as stencils (creating a shaped opening in the middle of the cardboard) and some as friskets (creating a solid piece of cardboard with outside edges that can be colored around).
2. Apply chalk on the edges of each shape.
3. Lay one shape on the background paper.
4. If the shape is a frisket, use a tissue to rub chalk from the shape outward onto the paper; use gentle sweeping motions. If the shape is a stencil, brush inward from the edge of the cardboard to the center of the opening.
5. Continue with the other shapes.
6. Shapes may be repeated until the page is filled.
7. Shapes may overlap, touch, merge, and so forth.
8. Spray with fixative. Be sure to use only in a well-ventilated area.

Concepts: Soft textural qualities of chalk; filling the page; rhythm and unity through repetition and progressive transition

Skills: Cutting; using chalk; creating and using stencils and friskets

34

FLOATING IN SPACE

▶ ## Suggested Materials

- 12" × 18" black or dark-colored paper
- Colored chalks or chalk pastels
- Fixative

▶ ## Directions

1. Sketch large, looped, connecting, and overlapping designs and shapes.
2. Color with chalk.
3. Accent edges of shapes with a second or third color for a three-dimensional look.
4. Spray with fixative. Be sure to use only in a well-ventilated area.

Concepts: Restful effect of curved lines and shapes; rhythm through progressive transition; three-dimensional effects of light colors on dark background, different-colored edges, and overlapping

Skills: Using chalk; using light values on dark backgrounds; using colors and overlapping to create a three-dimensional look

Chalks/Pastels

CHALK ANIMALS

▶ Suggested Materials

- Pets or animal pictures for motivation and reference
- 12" × 18" brown construction paper
- Pencils
- Colored chalks or chalk pastels
- Tissues
- Fixative

▶ Directions

1. Choose an animal to draw.
2. Draw the animal carefully with pencil on brown construction paper. Make the animal as large as possible.
3. Color the animal with chalk, using a pet or picture as a guide.
4. Blend and soften chalk with your fingers or a tissue.
5. Spray with fixative. Be sure to use only in a well-ventilated area.

Concepts: Soft, easily blended color qualities of chalk; knowledge of characteristics and proportions of animals

Skills: Drawing in light and dark on a middle value; drawing animals; using and blending chalk

Chalks/Pastels

CHALK BIRDS

▶ **Suggested Materials**

- Pet bird or bird pictures for motivation and reference
- Scrap paper
- Pencils
- 12" × 18" construction paper (black, dark blue, or brown)
- Colored chalks or chalk pastels
- Tissues
- Fixative

▶ **Directions**

1. Choose a bird to draw.
2. Practice drawing detailed parts of the bird with pencil and chalk on scrap paper before starting to draw an entire bird.
   - Wing
   - Head
   - Claw
   - Tail
3. Draw an entire bird carefully with pencil on dark paper. Make it as large as possible.
4. Color the bird with chalk, including as much detail as possible.
5. Rub chalk with a finger or a tissue to blend and soften the edges.
6. Spray with fixative. Be sure to use only in a well-ventilated area.

Concepts: Soft, easily blended color qualities of chalk; knowledge of characteristics and proportions of birds; light colors on dark background

Skills: Drawing with light colors on dark background; drawing birds; observing and doing studies of individual parts, using and blending chalk

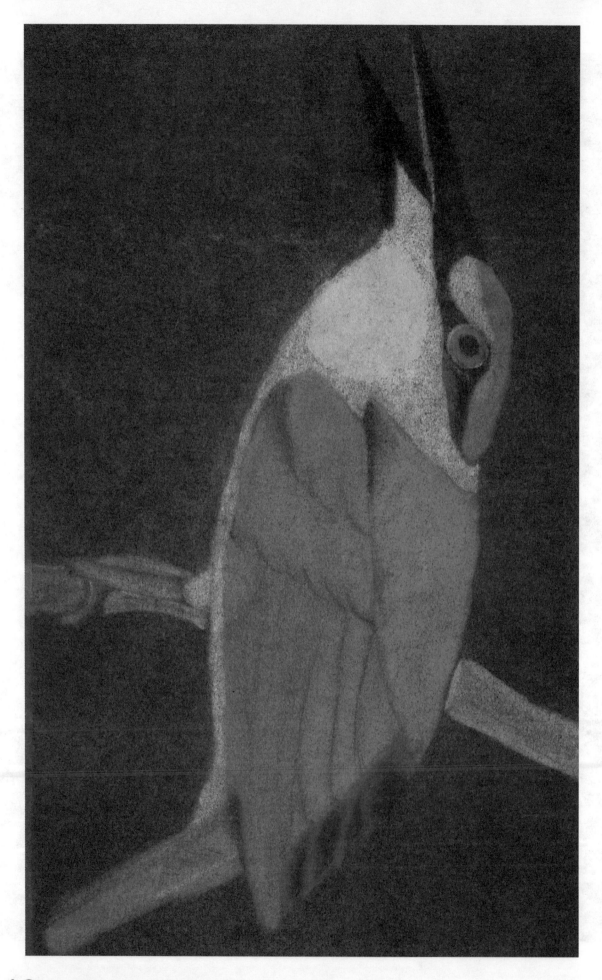

Chalks/Pastels

RAISED OUTLINE

▶ ## Suggested Materials

- Black or white paper
- Pencils
- Mixture of white glue plus black liquid tempera paint
- Colored chalks or chalk pastels
- Tissues or cotton swabs
- Fixative

Note: Use a bottle with a fine-point opening to hold the black glue. Be sure the glue and paint are mixed thoroughly. Provide one bottle per five or six students.

▶ ## Directions

1. Sketch a picture with pencil.
2. Starting at the top of the picture, re-draw lines slowly and carefully, using black-glue bottle.
3. Let dry thoroughly; black glue will form raised ridges.
4. Color with chalk; blend with your finger, a tissue, or a cotton swab. Black glue resists chalk and remains showing as black lines.
5. Spray with fixative. Be sure to use only in a well-ventilated area.

Concepts: Flexible use of media; variety; tendency of chalk to stay on rough paper and to be resisted by smooth glue lines

Skills: Using glue and paint in a new way

STILL-LIFE BOUQUET

▶ **Suggested Materials**

- Bouquet of multicolor flowers in vase
- 12" × 18" colored paper
- White tempera paint
- Brushes
- Colored chalks or chalk pastels

Note: Place the vase of flowers against a plain background where students can see it.

▶ **Directions**

1. Paint a picture of the vase of flowers with white paint. Leave open spaces where the background shows.
2. Let dry thoroughly.
3. Use colored chalk on top of the dried paint to color the flowers and vase and to add details.

Concepts: Positive and negative space; unity by shared color showing through; knowledge of flowers and leaves

Skills: Painting a silhouette shape to block out the art area; using chalk

White bouquet ready for
coloring with chalk

52

COLORED MARKERS/ CRAYONS

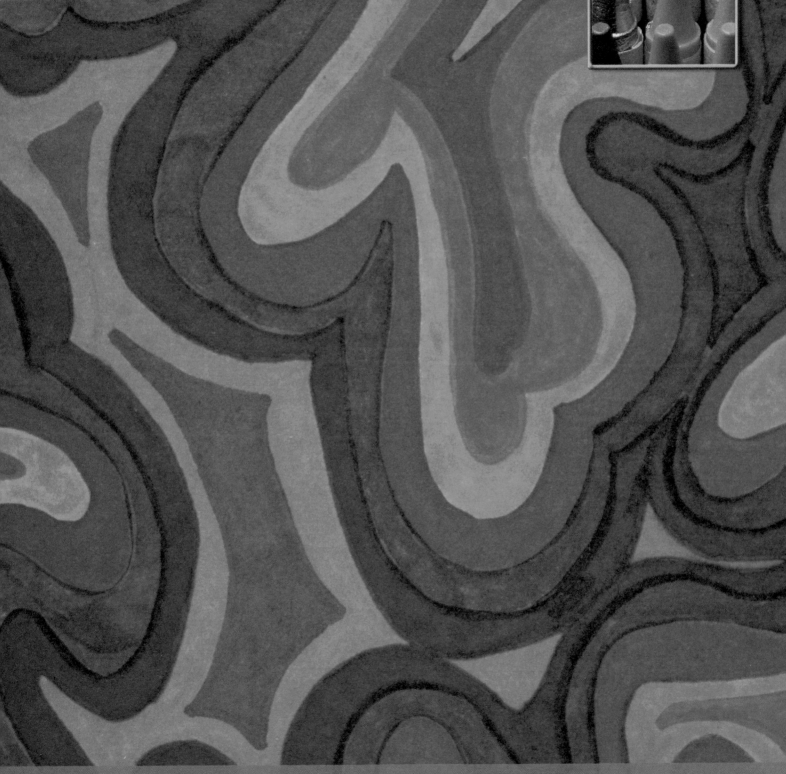

ILLUMINATED LETTERS

▶ Suggested Materials

- 12" × 18" white paper
- Pencils
- Colored markers or crayons
- Examples of Old English capitals or other elaborate letters

▶ Directions

Note: Before beginning work, discuss how illuminated (decorated) capital letters historically have been used to brighten pages of writing, especially during the Middle Ages.

1. Sketch a large, elaborate letter of the alphabet. Refer to examples if needed.

2. Decorate the interior of the letter and nearby open space. Decorations should be limited to one basic theme.

3. Color with markers or crayons. Select one set of colors for the letter and a different set of colors for the surrounding designs.

Concepts: Letters as art; historic use of illuminated capitals; unity through theme and colors; proportion

Skills: Drawing; coloring; decorating based on a theme

Colored Markers/Crayons

LOCKER OR CLOSET

▶ Suggested Materials

- 12" × 18" paper
- Pencils
- Crayons or colored markers

▶ Directions

1. Fold paper in half lengthwise.
2. Design the outside of the folded paper to be the front door of a locker or closet.
3. Open the door and design the inside. Be creative!
4. Color with markers or crayons.

Concepts: Proportion; unity with variety

Skills: Drawing; coloring; flexible and imaginative thinking; working in a long, thin format

Outside

Inside

T-SHIRT

▶ **Suggested Materials**

- Paper large enough for T-shirt pattern
- Pencils
- T-shirt patterns made from enlargement of pattern on next page
- Crayons or colored markers
- Scissors

▶ **Directions**

1. Think of three to five pictures to draw that reveal something about yourself (interests, spare-time activities, family, etc.).

2. Trace the T-shirt pattern on your paper.

3. Draw your name near the top of the shirt; use large, thick capital letters (for uniformity of size).

4. Add personal drawings. These should be simple, large drawings that overlap each other.

5. Outline with a thick black marker; color with bright crayons or markers.

6. Cut out the T-shirt.

7. Hang with clothespins on a line for display.

Concepts: Relating art with other personal interests; using several pictures together with type in one design; balance; emphasis through size, color, or position

Skills: Drawing; overlapping; coloring; choosing; arranging

T-shirt pattern to enlarge

Colored Markers/Crayons

BORDER DESIGNS

▶ Suggested Materials

- Pencils
- 6" × 9" scrap paper
- 6" × 9" tracing paper
- 12" × 18" paper
- Carbon paper
- Crayons or colored markers

▶ Directions

1. On 6" × 9" scrap paper draw a design to fill one corner and extend along both adjoining sides.

2. Trace your design onto tracing paper.

3. Place a sheet of carbon paper on top of one corner of a sheet of 12" × 18" paper. Place the 6" × 9" tracing paper design on top of the carbon paper, matching up the corner and two edges of the three layers of paper. Sketch over the design on the tracing paper so that the design is transferred through the carbon paper to the 12" × 18" paper.

4. Repeat the process in all the corners, turning the tracing paper around and over so that the design fits each corner properly to form a border.

5. Trace over lines with a black marker.

6. Color with markers or crayons.

7. If desired, use the center of the 12" × 18" paper for your name, a poem, a quote, or a Bible verse.

Concepts: Unity with variety; symmetrical balance; borders formed by repetition along edges

Skills: Drawing; tracing; using carbon paper to transfer a design; coloring; creating a border

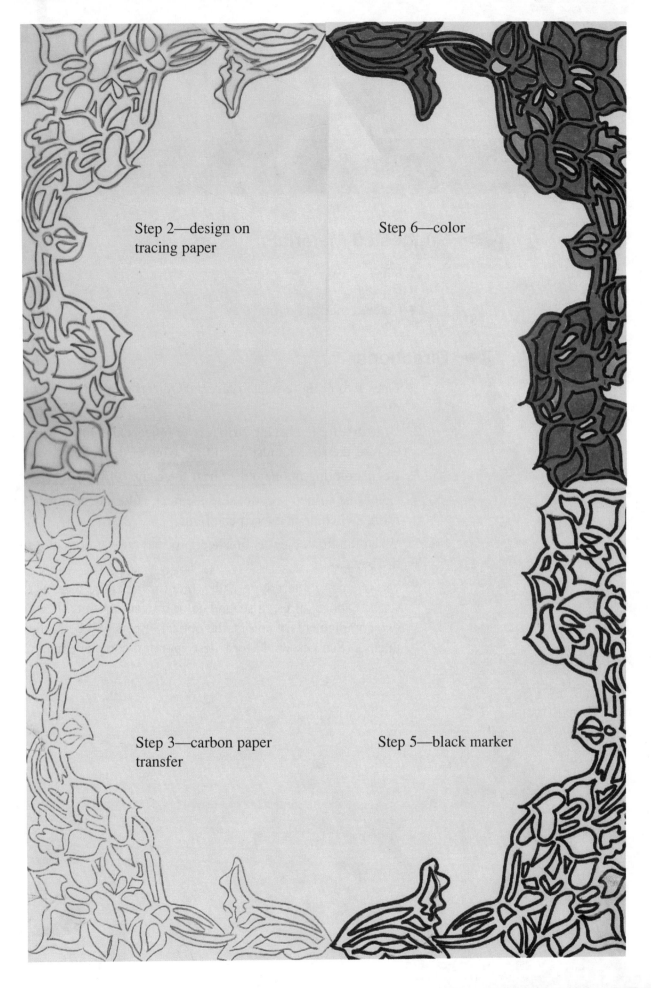

Step 2—design on
tracing paper

Step 6—color

Step 3—carbon paper
transfer

Step 5—black marker

STRIPED DESIGNS

▶ **Suggested Materials**

- Paper
- Pencils
- Colored markers or crayons

▶ **Directions**

1. Draw two or more related objects. Objects may touch but may not overlap.
2. Draw freeform, curving stripes over objects and entire paper. Both ends of the stripes must run off the edge of the paper.
3. Begin coloring in one object near the center of the paper.
4. Color one striped section, skip the next, color the next, and so forth, switching at every pencil line.
5. When the first object is finished, proceed outward to color the entire page.
6. Use one color alternating with white for the entire page as described above, or use a second color instead of white. If you use two complementary colors, the optical effects will be particularly intense. (See Lesson 47 for a description of complementary colors.)

Concepts: Pattern and rhythm through repetition and progressive transition; balance of positive and negative space; unity with variety; optical effects of colors placed side by side

Skills: Planning; arranging; drawing; coloring

PICTORIAL CALLIGRAPHY

▶ ## Suggested Materials

- Paper
- Pencils
- Crayons or colored markers

▶ ## Directions

To draw words that fill and form the shape of a subject:

1. Choose one of the following subjects: a geometric shape, an object, a creature, a plant, or a person.
2. Form the subject by using distorted letters of its name. Have the name of your subject fill the inside of the shape.
3. Color and decorate.

To draw words distorted to illustrate the meaning of a subject:

1. Select a word or words.
2. Distort letters so that they help convey the meaning of the word (e.g., melting or burning letters for the word *hot*).

Concepts: Words as art helping to convey their own meaning; emphasis through size, shape, and position; proportion

Skills: Imaginative thinking; arranging; drawing; coloring

A BIKE'S NEGATIVE SPACE

▶ **Suggested Materials**

- Bicycle (or any large, open object)
- 12" × 18" white paper
- Pencils
- Colored markers or crayons

Note: Set the bike on a table with a plain background behind it.

▶ **Directions**

1. With pencil draw a portion of the bike to fill the entire page, paying attention to details.

2. Trace over pencil lines with a black marker or crayon.

3. Leaving the bike parts white, use colored markers or crayons to fill the background spaces with various colors.

Concepts: Importance of filling the page and using negative space (the background space between shapes) as part of your design; balance; proportion

Skills: Observing details; selecting; planning; drawing; coloring

Colored Markers/Crayons

CLOWN FACES

► Suggested Materials

- Clown photographs
- Paper
- Pencils
- Colored markers or crayons

► Directions

Note: Display clown photographs and discuss their makeup, costumes, and reasons for performing.

1. Sketch a clown face; include hair, hat, and so forth.

2. Use a dark-colored (not black or brown) marker or crayon to go over all pencil lines. Make the lines thick.

3. Color the rest of the clown and background with bright colors.

Concepts: Flexible use of color; unity through common outline color; knowledge about clowns

Skills: Drawing basic face shapes; coloring

FIREWORKS

▶ Suggested Materials

- 9" × 12" white paper
- Colored markers or crayons

▶ Directions

1. Draw three to five marker or crayon dots randomly on paper.
2. Select a different color and draw short, evenly spaced rays extending from the dots.
3. Continue drawing rays with different colors until the paper is filled.
4. Circles will run into and merge with each other.

Concepts: Filling the page; pattern, unity, and rhythm through repetition and progressive transition; proportion

Skills: Planning; arranging; coloring

Colored Markers/Crayons

FRYING PAN ART

▶ Suggested Materials

- Old electric frying pan
- Crayon scraps
- Paper—approximately 6" × 9"
- 9" × 12" or larger paper
- Newspaper or paper towels

Note: Heat the pan to 250 degrees.

▶ Directions

Note: With younger students, the teacher should do the second step in order to avoid burns. For older students, teacher supervision may be sufficient.

1. Rub or drop crayon scraps (single color or variety) in desired spots on the bottom of the pan and let the wax melt.
2. Drag small pieces of paper across the melted wax.
3. Lay the papers flat to cool (page 83).
4. Cut shapes from the cooled wax papers and use with other media for designing a picture on the larger paper (pages 84-85).

Note: Clean the pan by wiping out excess crayon with newspaper or paper towels.

Concepts: Qualities of wax crayons; creative use of "scrap" sizes of crayons and paper; combining different media and techniques in one design

Skills: Using crayons; cutting; imaginative thinking and combination of media and techniques

84

DIAGONAL DESIGNS

▶ Suggested Materials

- White paper
- Pencils
- Rulers
- Wide-tip black markers
- Colored markers or crayons

▶ Directions

1. Use a ruler and black marker to draw diagonal lines on the paper. Each line may run off the edge of the paper or end at another line. (This could be done with pencil first to lessen mistakes.)

2. Use colored markers or crayons to draw rays of color extending from the corners of the page and corners formed by lines.

Concepts: Active, exciting effect of diagonal lines; filling the page

Skills: Using rulers; using markers or crayons; arranging

GRID DRAWING

▶ ## Suggested Materials

- Small pictures to enlarge
- Transparent acetate (optional)
- Pencils
- Rulers or yardsticks
- 12" × 18" paper
- Colored markers or crayons

▶ ## Directions

Note: Although the directions in this lesson are for making an enlarged copy, this same process can be used to make smaller or same-sized copies of almost any picture.

1. To make a large copy of a small picture, mark a pencil grid on the original picture or on a sheet of transparent acetate placed over the original. Mark the grid by making dots at regular, measured intervals along the sides; then connect the dots across the picture with a ruler.

2. Mark a pencil grid with the same number of (larger) squares on 12" × 18" paper.

3. Observe what is in each square on the small picture and reproduce it on the large paper.

4. Continue until all squares are completed.

5. Erase the grid marks; color with colored markers or crayons.

Concepts: Copying, enlarging, or reducing a complex drawing by dividing it into smaller, simpler parts

Skills: Drawing a proportionately enlarged copy by the grid method; using rulers; coloring

Step 1—grid over original

Step 2—enlarged grid

Steps 3 and 4—enlarged art

Colored Markers/Crayons

Step 5—final colored art

SYMMETRICAL DESIGNS

▶ ## Suggested Materials

- 12" × 12" white paper
- Pencils
- Rulers
- Compasses
- Colored markers or crayons
- Wide-tip black markers
- Newspaper

▶ ## Directions

Note: Discuss radial symmetry—design must be the same when viewed from any side.

1. Locate the center of the paper by connecting the opposite corners with two faint lines. The point at which the two lines cross is the exact center.

2. Begin drawing a design in the center and work outward. The design is divided into fourths, so each fourth must be exactly the same to be symmetrical.

3. Whenever one line is drawn, it must be drawn again in the exact same place in the other three-fourths of the design.

4. Keep spaces small. The more lines and spaces, the better.

5. When the entire paper is adequately filled with the design, trace the lines with a wide-tip black marker and a ruler.

6. Lay a thick newspaper cushion underneath the paper when coloring.

7. Color spaces heavily with marker or crayon. Remember, there must be four of each design space (one in each fourth of the page) and all four must be colored the same color.

Note: A slightly more difficult variation would be to create the design within a large circle filling the paper. Cut out the circle when finished. (See examples on page 95.)

Concepts: Balance through radial symmetry (symmetrical arrangement around a center point); unity; proportion

Skills: Planning; measuring; arranging; using rulers and compasses; using markers or crayons

Colored Markers/Crayons

FALLING OBJECTS

▶ Suggested Materials

- 12" × 18" white paper
- Pencils
- Rulers or yardsticks
- Scrap paper
- Scissors (optional)
- Black markers
- Colored markers or crayons

▶ Directions

Note: For younger students, leave out steps 6 and 7. (See example on page 100.)

1. Draw two horizontal lines about 2" apart down the center of the 18" length of the paper (to represent a street).

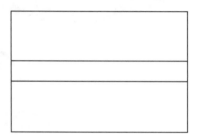

2. On each 18" edge of the paper (above and below the street lines), draw five to seven rectangles (building roofs) of different sizes. They may extend off the edges of the paper and may be next to each other.

3. Draw a dot for the VP (vanishing point) in the center of the street near the center of the paper.

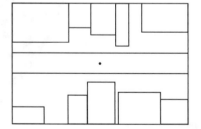

Concepts: Introducing the concept of lines converging toward a vanishing point; understanding that smaller objects in art appear to be farther away

Skills: Drawing; using rulers; coloring; creating the appearance of one-point linear perspective

4. Draw lines from the VP to the corners of the rectangles closest to the street (forming front walls of buildings facing the street). If a line would cross another building, leave out the part of it that would cross the building.

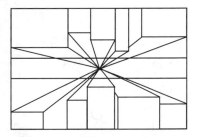

5. Erase portions of lines within the street.

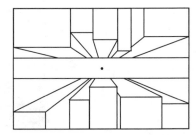

6. Draw windows and doors on the front walls. Side lines of windows and doors need to line up with the VP. Tops and bottoms of the windows need to be parallel to the street.

7. Add details to the buildings and roofs. If desired, add windows and doors to the side walls of the buildings also.

8. On scrap paper, draw a falling object in different sizes and positions.

9. Trace (or cut out and draw around) the smallest falling objects near the VP and largest objects near the outer edge of the paper.

10. Erase building lines within the objects.

11. Retrace the entire drawing with black markers.

12. Color falling objects with vivid colors.

Colored Markers/Crayons

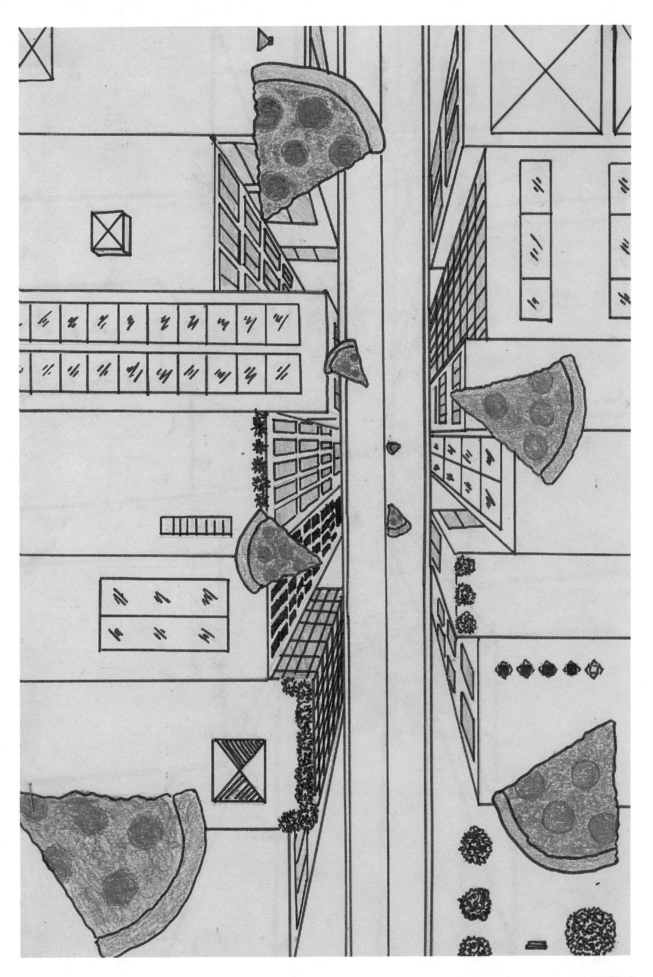

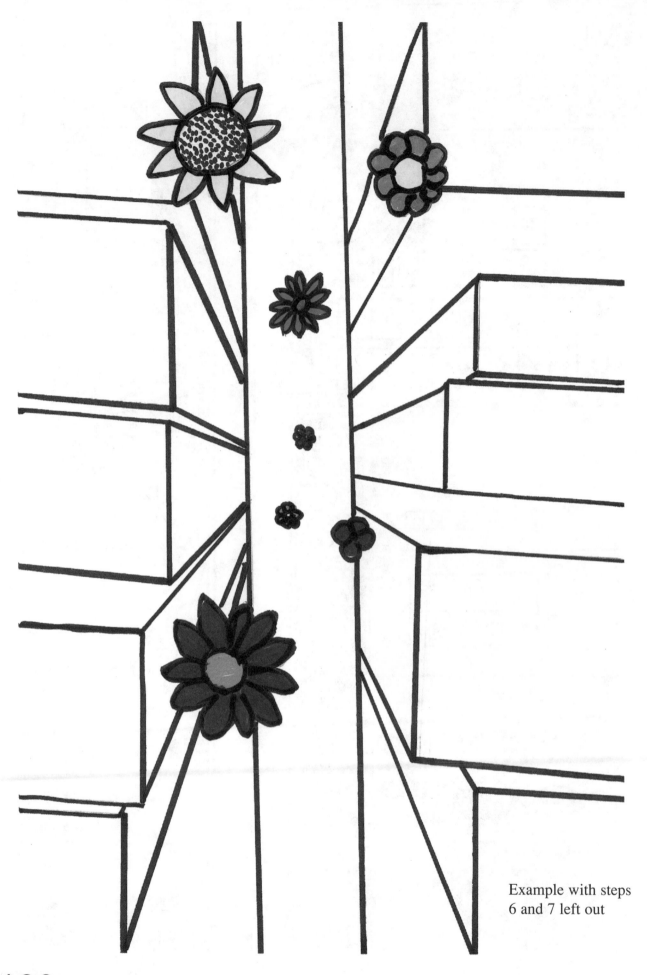

Example with steps
6 and 7 left out

TWO-POINT PERSPECTIVE

▶ Suggested Materials

- 12" × 18" white paper
- Pencils
- Rulers or yardsticks at least 18" long
- Colored markers or crayons

▶ Directions

1. Draw a dot for the VP (vanishing point) near the middle of each 12" edge of the paper.

2. Draw an 8" vertical line near the center of the paper. This line will be the corner where two sides of a flat-top building meet closest to the viewer.

3. Draw lines connecting the top and bottom of the 8" vertical line to the VPs to form two walls of a building.

4. Draw a vertical line on each side to end the walls. Erase extra parts of the diagonal lines but do not erase the VPs.

5. Draw a horizontal line through the VPs; leave out the part of the line that crosses the walls. This line will divide the ground from the sky.

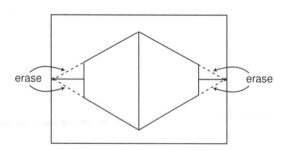

6. All horizontal lines to the left of the 8" vertical line will line up with the left VP.

7. All horizontal lines to the right of the 8" vertical line will line up with the right VP.

8. Sides of building, doors, windows, and so forth are ALWAYS vertical.

9. Add sidewalks, curbs, and streets. You may also add shrubs and trees. Trace over or color with crayons or markers.

Concepts: Things farther away from us appear to be smaller; introducing the concept of two-point perspective with lines converging toward two vanishing points at eye level on the horizon

Skills: Drawing; using rulers; coloring; creating the appearance of two-point linear perspective

Colored Markers/Crayons

CREATURE WANTED!

▶ Suggested Materials

- Paper
- Pencils (optional)
- Crayons or colored markers
- Photo of an unfamiliar and unusual creature

Note: Prepare a description of the creature to read to your students. Do not show the photo until after the students have finished their drawings.

▶ Directions

1. Your teacher will read a description of an unusual creature.
2. Draw the creature without looking at the photo of it; do not look at other students' drawings or ask questions.
3. Afterwards compare your results with the drawings of others and with the photograph of the real creature.

▶ Suggested Reading

Note: If you use this specific example, do not let your students view this photograph until after they have drawn their pictures.

I saw a creature the other day, and I wonder if you've seen it? Let's make "wanted poster" pictures so that we can find it.

- It has a large body shaped like a flat balloon that is orange on one side, light red on the other, and black along part of the edge.
- It has shiny black, irregularly shaped spots on its body.
- It has a small oblong head that is orange, red, and black like its body.
- It has six shiny black legs and two black antennae.

Note: Later, have students write descriptions of creatures that others could draw.

Concepts: Appreciating the value of visual art and photographs since verbal or written information may be interpreted differently by different people

Skills: Imaginative thinking; drawing from a verbal description

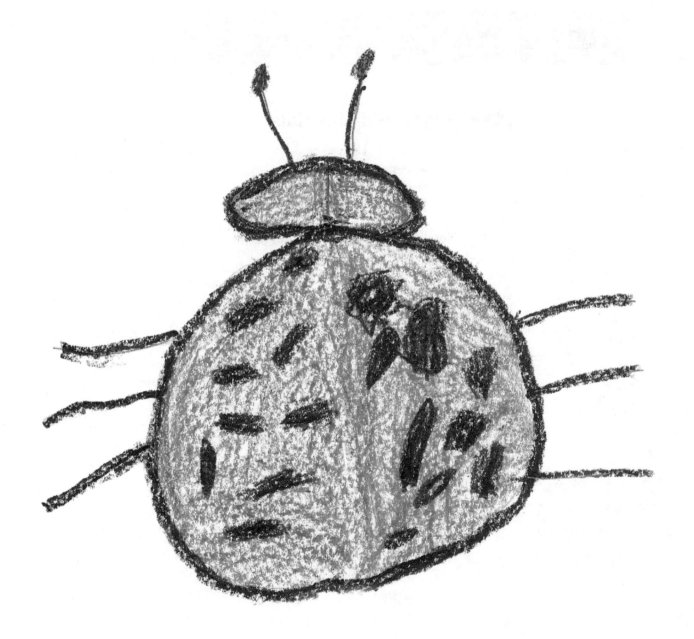

EGYPTIAN ART

▶ **Suggested Materials**

- 12" × 18" paper
- Pencils
- Crayons or colored markers
- Photographs of Egyptian art (optional)

Note: Review the information on the next page about Egyptian art before reading to your students.

▶ **Directions**

1. Your teacher will read information about Egyptian art and its rules.

2. Look at photos of Egyptian art, if available.

3. Draw an Egyptian figure on your paper. Since Egyptian figures generally face toward the hieroglyphics that go with them, and the hieroglyphic symbols face in that same direction, make the figure face left. Leave room down the left side of the page to write your name in hieroglyphics.

4. Write your name in hieroglyphics (see page 110) along the left side (the side that the figure faces).

5. Color, using the following colors only, which were the colors the Egyptians used:
   - Red
   - Yellow
   - Green
   - Blue
   - Black
   - White
   - Brown

Concepts: Art reflecting the culture and the religious beliefs of the artist; knowledge of ancient Egyptian art and hieroglyphics

Skills: Drawing; coloring; writing name in hieroglyphics

►ART OF THE ANCIENT EGYPTIANS

The religious beliefs of the ancient Egyptians affected all aspects of their life and art. The Egyptians did not believe in one true God; they believed in several main gods and goddesses and hundreds of lesser gods, many of which were represented by animals. They built impressive temples as the homes of gods, funeral chapels of pharaohs (rulers who were thought to be the sky god Horus in human form), and small models of the universe. They also believed in an afterlife in a world much like Egypt. One would be allowed to enter that world if his heart (bearing a record of all his past deeds) proved pure enough when weighed on a scale against the "feather of truth." They believed that the soul (or *ka*) left the body at death but eventually returned to rejoin it (or, if necessary, an image of it) for the journey to the afterlife. If the body was destroyed and there was no substitute image, the *ka* would wander hopelessly forever.

In order to protect their dead bodies, all Egyptians who could afford to do so built tombs of solid stone in dry places near the edge of the desert. In addition, the bodies were preserved by embalming and wrapping. The wrapped bodies, called mummies, were put in special decorated cases. Frequently, statues or paintings of the person were also placed in the tomb for the *ka* to enter if anything happened to the body. The walls of tombs and temples were covered with pictures and hieroglyphics showing the daily activities, relatives, friends, and servants of the dead person. The Egyptians believed that prayers by the priests could cause the god Osiris to bring these people back to life. The tomb also held food, jewelry, and personal objects for the dead person.

For thousands of years Egyptian art followed strict rules. Although the art looks strange to us today, the rules' purpose was that parts of a body or object would be shown in their most familiar and complete point of view. In pictures of people, the head, hips, legs, and feet were always shown in profile view, while the eye and shoulders were in front view. Distinguishing features, such as thumbs, foot arches, and big toes were included on both hands or feet regardless of whether they could actually be seen. If the scene or person came to life again, nothing important would be incomplete.

Other Egyptian rules for art controlled size, arrangement, and color. Size of a person indicated importance rather than actual size. Artists arranged parts of a picture neatly in horizontal rows with things that were actually behind being placed above to be clearly visible. Sometimes different parts of a story were arranged along horizontal bands. Artists used few colors and made them bright and flat (not shaded). Egyptian men were painted reddish brown, women golden brown, and most slaves darker brown.

Another important aspect of Egyptian art was hieroglyphic writing. Some symbols represented words, some sounds, and some clues to the meaning of words. People writing in hieroglyphics today have to think in sounds, not letters, since the symbols do not always represent exactly the same sounds as modern letters. Also, Egyptian scribes sometimes left out vowel sounds, so spelling can be confusing. Hieroglyphics could be written left to right, right to left, or top to bottom, and the symbols could be arranged in many different ways to make the writing fit and look attractive in its space.

HIEROGLYPHIC ALPHABET

A

B

C Use K or S.

CH/TH

D

E

F

G
For *g* as in *gentle,* use J.

H or

I

J

K

L

M

N

O

P

Q

R

S
For *s* as in *please,* use Z.

SH

T

U/W

V Use F.

X Use KS.

Y
For *y* as in *happy,* use E.

Z

MY HOUSE

▶ Suggested Materials

- 12" × 18" white paper
- Pencils
- Rulers
- Crayons or markers

▶ Directions

Note: Prior to the lesson, encourage students to observe carefully the front of their homes or apartments.

1. Draw the front view of your own home or apartment building.
2. Color with markers or crayons.

Concepts: Knowledge about homes (structure, variety, proportions, colors, etc.)

Skills: Observing; drawing; coloring; using rulers

Colored Markers/Crayons

PENCILS/
COLORED PENCILS

3 LESSONS ▶

SHOE DRAW

▶ **Suggested Materials**

- Student's shoe
- Paper
- Pencils
- Colored pencils (optional)

▶ **Directions**

1. Remove one shoe and place it on your desk.
2. Observing very carefully, draw the shoe exactly as it looks.
3. The drawing may be shaded or colored.

Concepts: Seeing beneath surface appearances to find order and beauty in everyday subjects; knowledge about shoes

Skills: Observing; drawing

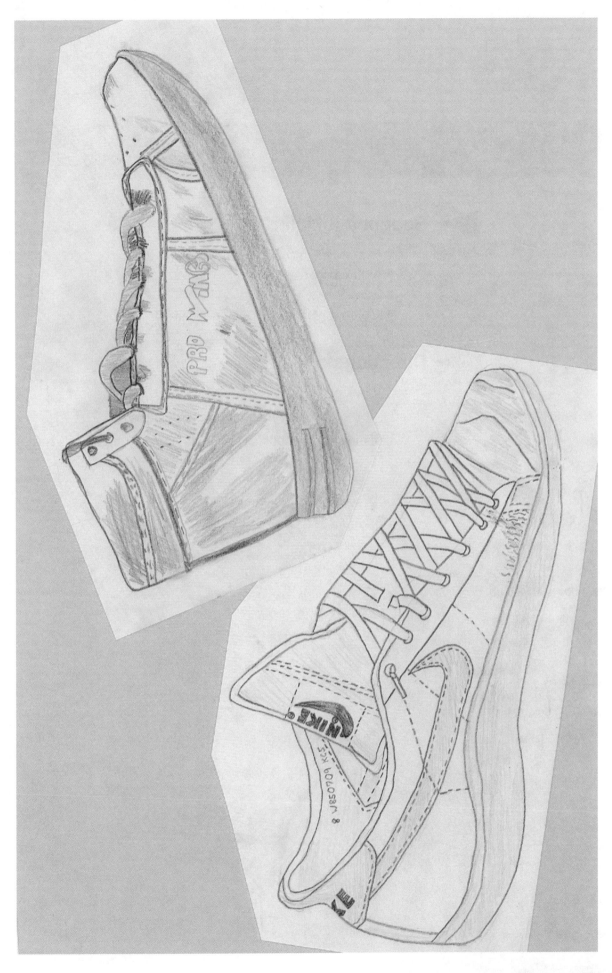

SPECIAL CARS

▶ Suggested Materials

- Car photos from brochures or magazines
- White paper
- Pencils
- Colored pencils

▶ Directions

1. Look at car photos or real cars.
2. Draw a car, paying attention to details.
3. Color with pencils, shading and creating highlights for the shine.

Concepts: Knowledge about the appearance of cars; qualities of colored pencils

Skills: Observing details; drawing; using colored pencils

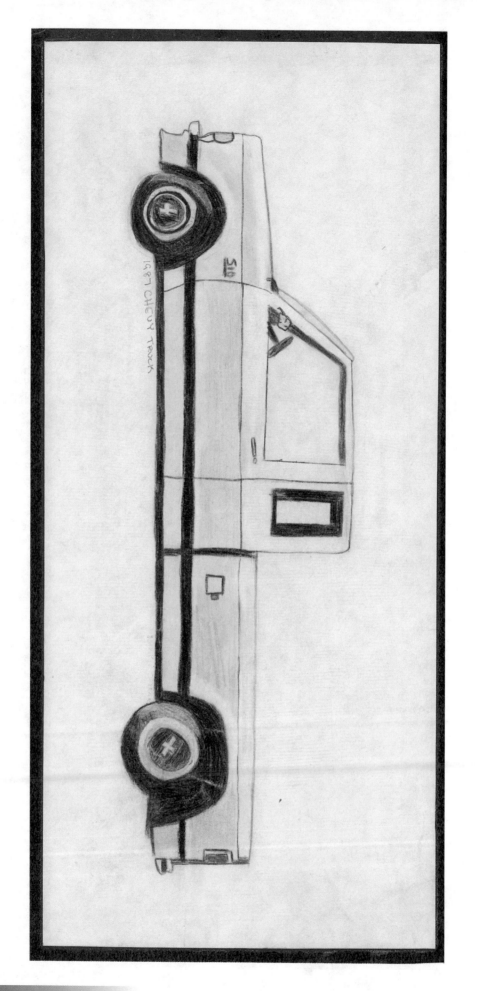

Pencils/Colored Pencils

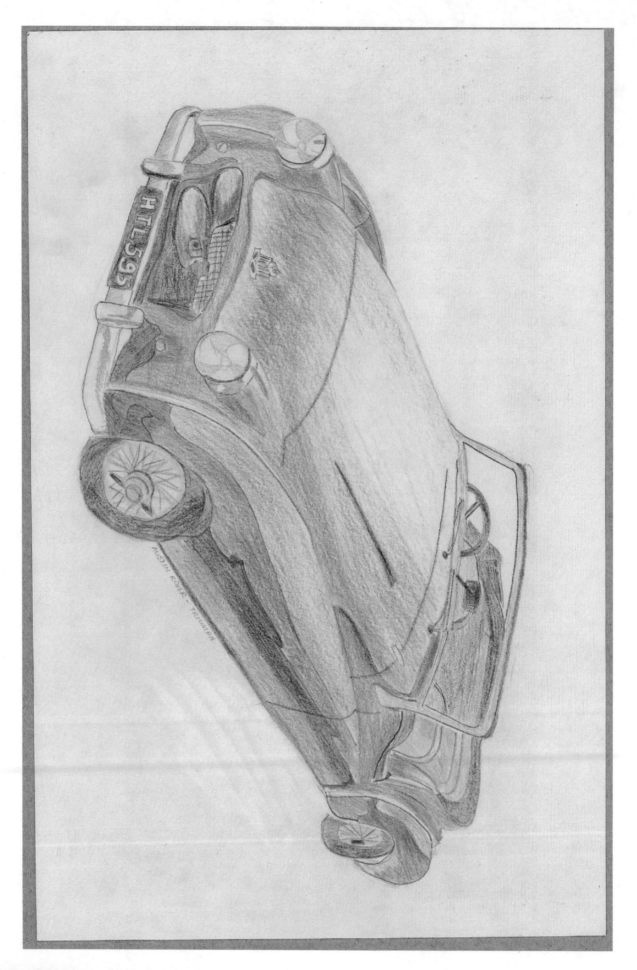

Pencils/Colored Pencils

DREAM SUITE

▶ Suggested Materials

- Graph paper
- Pencils
- Rulers

▶ Directions

1. Make a list of things you would include in a dream suite if cost did not matter.

2. Obtain approximate measurements and sizes of furniture and appliances at home or in stores and record these on the list.

3. Begin your floor plan by choosing a scale (1 square = ? feet). (1 square = 1 foot is easiest.)

4. Draw your floor plan in pencil on a sheet of graph paper. Include doors and windows. Walls, doors, and windows should be drawn with double lines and then shaded.

5. Add all furnishings using approximate measurements. Label everything.

Concepts: Scale drawing; floor plans; knowledge of furniture and appliance sizes and arrangement

Skills: Drawing to scale; planning; arranging

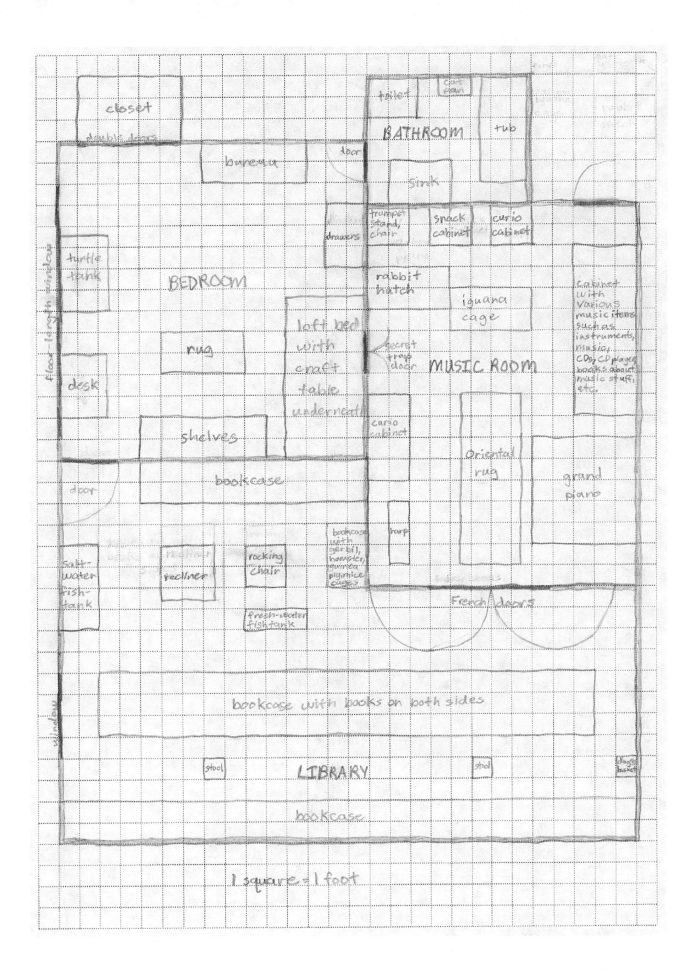

closet

double doors

bureau

BATHROOM

toilet

tub

door

sink

turtle tank

BEDROOM

drawers

trumpet stand, chair

snack cabinet

curio cabinet

rabbit hatch

iguana cage

cabinet with various music items such as instruments, music, CDs, CD player, books about music stuff, etc.

rug

loft bed with craft table underneath

secret trap door

MUSIC ROOM

desk

shelves

curio cabinet

Oriental rug

grand piano

door

bookcase

harp

salt-water fish-tank

recliner

recliner

rocking chair

bookcase with gerbil, hamster, guinea pig, mice cages

French doors

fresh-water fishtank

window

bookcase with books on both sides

stool

LIBRARY

stool

dog's basket

bookcase

1 square = 1 foot

CUT OR TORN PAPER

9 LESSONS ►

MAGAZINE MONTAGE

▶ Suggested Materials

- Old magazines
- Scissors
- 12" × 18" paper
- Glue

▶ Directions

1. Cut out interesting shapes, colors, and textures from magazine photographs.
2. Arrange cut pieces as a "face" on your paper.
3. Glue the pieces down.

Concepts: Visual texture; thinking about shapes, colors, and textures rather than subject; variety

Skills: Cutting; planning; arranging; gluing

CUT PAPER TEXTURES

▶ ## Suggested Materials

- Pencils
- 12" × 18" paper
- Colored paper
- Scissors
- White glue
- Bright spray paint (optional)

▶ ## Directions

1. Sketch outline shape of a bird, fish, insect, or another animal on 12" × 18" paper.

2. Cut colored paper shapes or use other media to color or prepare the background as desired.

3. From colored paper, cut many pointed ovals to use as feathers, fur, hair, or scales. Begin with rectangles approximately 1" × 3/4". Fold in half lengthwise. Cut as shown. Open the fold.

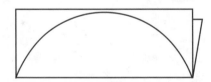

4. Glue the ovals down at one end but allow the other end to stand out—away from the background paper. Fill the outline shape with the ovals to create the effect of feathers, fur, hair, or scales.

5. Use cut colored paper to add legs, beak, eyes, and so forth.

6. If desired, protect background and spray bright paint over a few selected areas for additional interest.

Note: Be sure to cover clothes and surrounding area to protect from spray paint. Use paint in a well-ventilated area only.

Concepts: Texture of subject suggested three-dimensionally by materials and technique

Skills: Cutting; arranging; gluing; patience; orderly work

Cut or Torn Paper

PERSONALIZED PERSON

▶ Suggested Materials

- 12" × 18" paper
- Pencils
- Rulers
- Colored pencils
- Scissors
- Glue
- "Junk" box of foil, yarn, beads, fabric, trim, and so forth
- Scrap paper

▶ Directions

1. Fold a sheet of 12" × 18" paper in half the long way.

2. Use a pencil and ruler to draw lines 1/4" from the folded edge and from the 18" cut edge of the paper.

3. With the folded edge at the bottom, write (in cursive) your name. Use first or last name, initial and last name, or both names (whatever best fills the length of the paper). Use the pencil line near the folded edge as your writing line with the line near the open edges as the top of your tallest letters. Leave off tails of letters *f, g, j, p, q, y,* and *z,* which would go below the writing line.

4. Be sure all letters are connected.

5. Widen the letters to 1/2" in width (thickness). To obtain the 1/2" thickness, use a colored pencil to widen the letters 1/4" on each side of the original marking of the letters. This will make the word fill the entire width of the folded paper.

6. Leaving the paper folded, cut on colored lines to remove the background, leaving the name intact. Be sure to cut out openings in the letters as well.

7. Unfold the name and glue it down on a 12" × 18" sheet of contrasting paper. Glue the side the pencil lines are on.

8. Decorate your name as a character by adding items from the "junk" box or pieces of scrap paper cut into designs or objects.

Concepts: Balance through bilateral symmetry (same on both sides of a center line); using words and "junk" items creatively as parts of art

Skills: Cutting; planning; flexible thinking; gluing

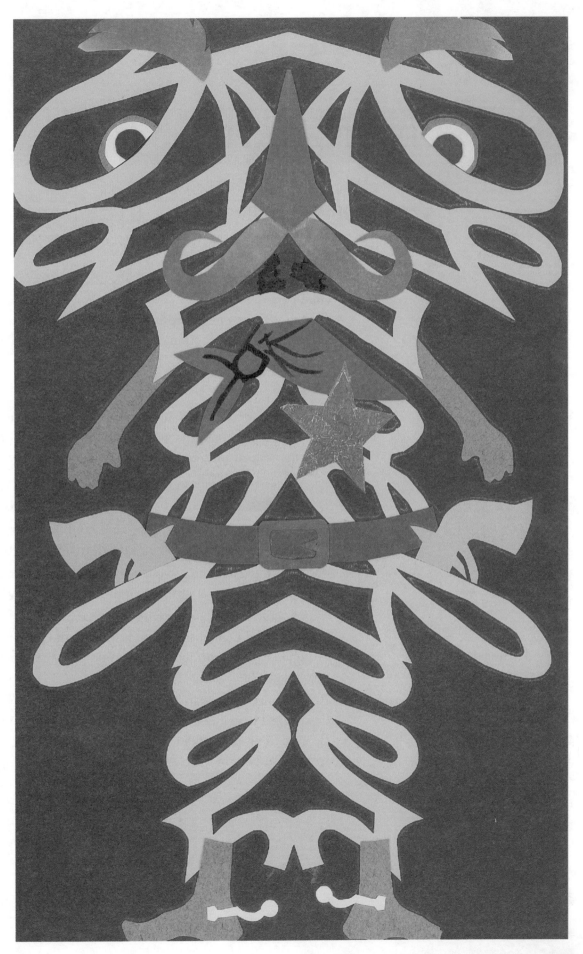

POSITIVE-NEGATIVE

Concepts: Importance in design of both positive and negative space; pattern and rhythm through repetition; unity of treatment with variety of shapes

Skills: Planning; cutting; arranging; gluing

▶ Suggested Materials

- 4 1/2" × 12" paper strips (black or a second color)
- Pencils
- Scissors
- Glue
- 9" × 12" white or colored paper
- Bright spray paint (optional)

▶ Directions

Note: For older students more than one strip may also be used. (See page 139, where three narrower strips were used; only one side of each of the outer two strips was cut; the center strip, of a third color, was left uncut.)

1. Draw designs on both long edges of a 4 1/2" × 12" strip of paper. Designs should start at the edge of the paper and go inward.

2. Cut out designs carefully, preserving both the design shapes and the background. Lay the shapes down in a systematic order.

3. After setting aside the cut-out designs, glue the remainder of the original 4 1/2" × 12" strip down the center of the 9" × 12" paper.

4. Match the cut-out designs with their corresponding holes in the original strip. Glue the cut-out designs to the left or right of the original strip. The arrangement should give the appearance of open pages of a book.

5. Bright spray paint (e.g., hot pink, fluorescent orange) accents may be spritzed here and there for added impact and color if desired. Be sure to protect clothes and the surrounding area from over-spray. Use only in a well-ventilated area.

Cut or Torn Paper

Example using three strips

QUILTING BEE

▶ Suggested Materials

- 9" × 9" white or colored paper
- Pencils
- Rulers
- Colored 6" × 9" paper printed with design pieces (see next page). Provide two per student.
- Scissors
- Glue

▶ Directions

1. On 9" × 9" paper, use a pencil and a ruler to draw very light lines, as shown, to connect opposite corners and centers of opposite sides. This will help you place your "quilt pieces" symmetrically.

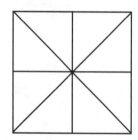

2. Cut out design pieces very carefully.
3. Arrange pieces in a symmetrical design on 9" × 9" paper. The design must look the same from all four sides.
4. If you need more small pieces, cut larger pieces in half.
5. Glue pieces down.
6. A group of designs may be displayed side by side on a bulletin board, forming one giant quilt.

Concepts: Importance in design of both positive and negative space; balance through radial symmetry (symmetrical arrangement around a center point); unity

Skills: Planning; arranging; cutting; gluing

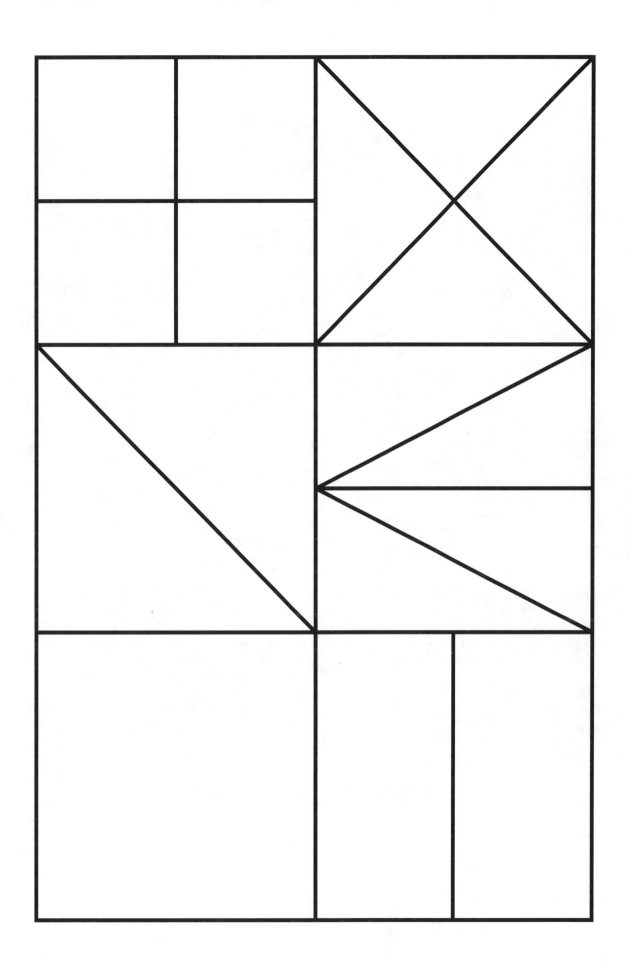

Cut or Torn Paper

SIXTEEN-PIECE FIGURES

▶ Suggested Materials

- Scrap paper (colored)
- Background paper
- Glue

▶ Directions

Note: Discuss and observe the shapes and relative sizes of the parts of the human figure and where and in what directions the figure can bend.

1. Tear sixteen pieces of colored paper for each figure. Try to make them the appropriate shapes and relative sizes of the parts of the human figure. The pieces will be used for the head, neck, upper body, lower body, two forearms, two upper arms, two hands, two upper legs, two lower legs, and two feet.

2. Lay the pieces down on the background paper and assemble them in an action position.

3. Glue pieces to the background when they are positioned correctly.

Concepts: Knowledge of the proportions and parts of the human figure and how those parts move when in action

Skills: Observing and showing action; tearing; arranging; gluing

Cut or Torn Paper

STRETCHED PICTURES

► Suggested Materials

- 9" × 12" paper
- Pencils
- Scissors
- Glue

► Directions

1. Draw an object or an animal.
2. Draw light pencil lines to divide it into sections or parts.
3. Cut the sections apart; keep them in systematic order.
4. Glue the pieces onto a background sheet, leaving small even spaces between sections.

Concepts: Unity through making the background part of the subject

Skills: Planning; drawing; cutting; gluing

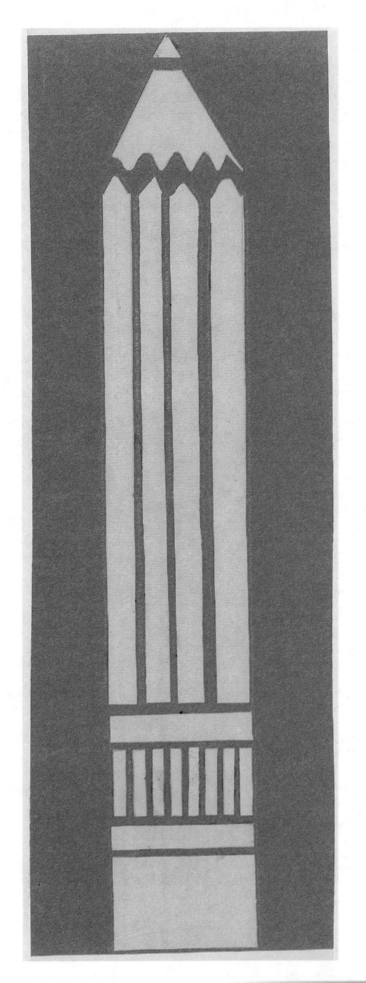

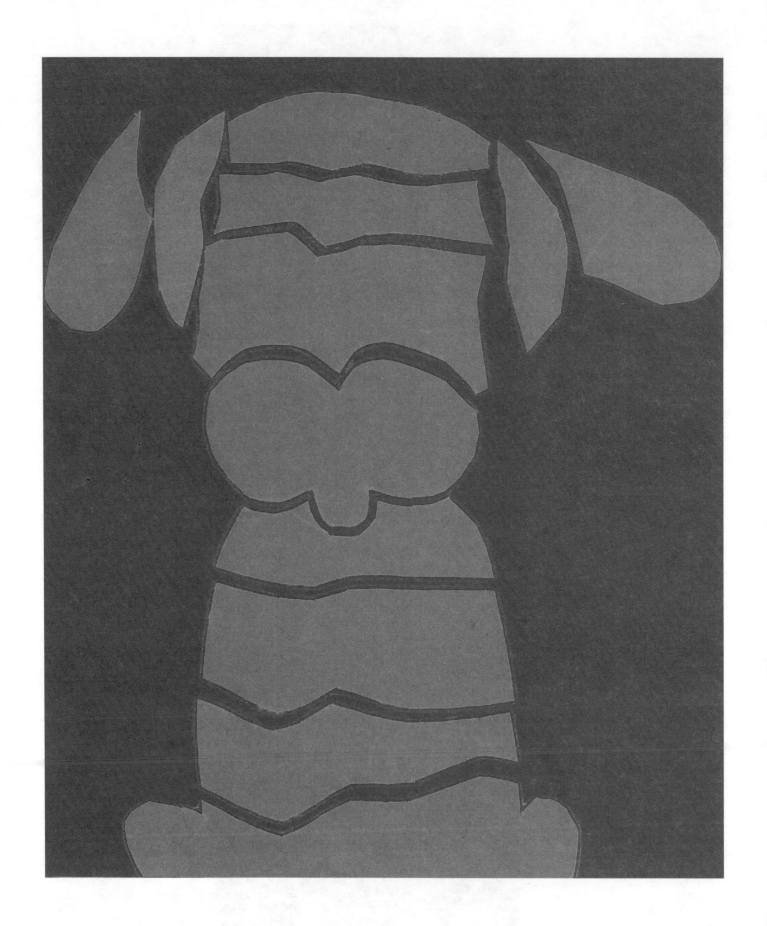

Cut or Torn Paper

TORN FIGURES

► Suggested Materials

- Paper
- Glue
- Crayons or markers (optional)

► Directions

1. Observe a model in an active pose.
2. Carefully tear the shape of a human figure in that pose from a piece of paper.
3. Glue to a background piece of contrasting paper.
4. If desired, draw background details with crayons or markers.

Concepts: Knowledge of the proportions and parts of the human figure and how those parts move when in action

Skills: Observing and showing action; tearing; gluing

DOILY DOLLIES

▶ Suggested Materials

- Paper doilies
- White scrap paper
- Colored paper
- Scissors
- Glue

▶ Directions

1. Using colored paper for the background, construct a doll from white paper and doilies in the position desired.

2. Cut and shape pieces from white paper and doilies for accents, hair, features on face, and so forth.

3. Paper can be cut, folded, scored, curled, and so forth.

4. Attempt to glue parts in place so that they stand "up" and "away from" the background in order to create a three-dimensional look.

Concepts: Form; pattern; three-dimensional relief paper sculpture; using materials in creative ways

Skills: Planning; cutting; folding; scoring; curling; gluing

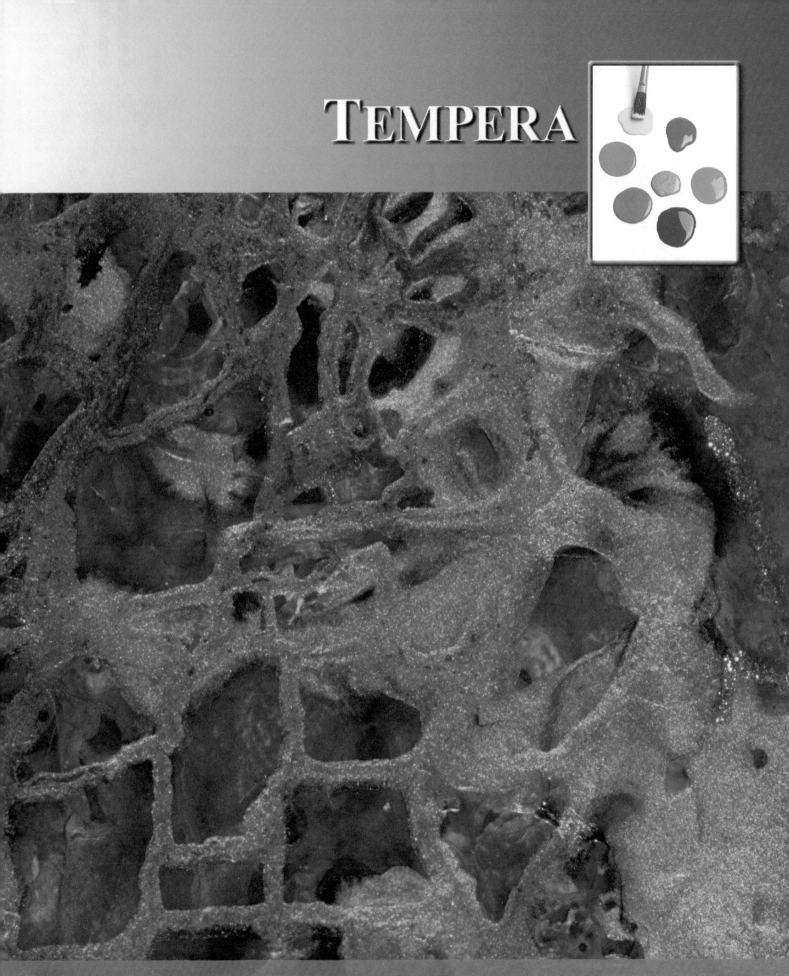

TEMPERA

COLOR WHEEL

▶ Suggested Materials

- Color wheel worksheets, one for each student (copy page 161)
- Pencils
- Crayons
- Tempera paint—red, yellow, and blue
- Brushes
- 12" × 18" white drawing paper
- Containers of water for cleaning brushes
- 12" × 12" white drawing paper
- Compass (or plate to trace around)
- Scissors
- Glue
- Colored markers

▶ Directions

Color Wheel Worksheet

Note: See the teacher key on page 160 to guide the students as they complete their worksheets.

1. On your worksheet, label the three largest circles with the names of the primary colors. Label the other circles with the names of the colors formed by mixing the primary colors. Color the circles with the corresponding colors of crayon.

2. List the three primary colors (yellow, red, blue).

3. List the three secondary colors (orange, violet, green).

4. Define complementary colors as the colors located directly across the wheel from each other (like the spokes in a wheel). Examples: yellow across from violet, yellow orange across from blue violet, orange across from blue, and so forth. Complementary colors enhance each other when placed close to one another. For example, if you were doing a bulletin board with a blue background, orange would be a good color choice for the lettering. However, if complementary colors are mixed together, they neutralize, or gray, one another.

Concepts: Color wheel; primary, secondary, and complementary colors

Skills: Color mixing; cutting; gluing

Painted Color Wheel

1. Fold a sheet of 12" × 18" paper into sixteen small rectangles.

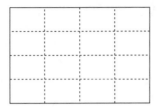

2. Using a brush and the three primary colors of paint, mix and paint the thirteen colors listed below in thirteen of the sixteen rectangles.

Note: Due to the properties of the red, yellow, and blue tempera paints, some colors may be a little harder than others to create by mixing.

- yellow
- yellow + touch of red = yellow orange
- yellow + red = orange
- yellow + more red = red orange
- Clean brush
  - red
  - red + touch of blue = red violet
  - red + blue = violet or purple
  - red + more blue = blue violet
- Clean brush
  - yellow + touch of blue = yellow green (lime)
  - yellow + blue = green
  - yellow + more blue = blue green
- Clean brush
  - blue
  - red + blue + yellow = neutral gray-brown

3. Draw simple shapes with a pencil in the remaining three spaces.

4. When the paint has dried thoroughly, trace the outline of your favorite shape on the back of each painted rectangle.

5. Following your trace marks, cut out the thirteen painted shapes. Using your worksheet as a guide, glue the first twelve in order in a large circle on 12" × 12" paper. (Use a compass or trace around a plate to form a circle.)

6. Connect the primary colors with a solid black marker line.

7. Connect the secondary colors with a dotted black marker line.

8. Connect each pair of complementary colors with a light-colored marker line (yellow or orange).

9. Glue the neutral gray-brown shape in the center.

THE COLOR WHEEL
(Teacher Key)

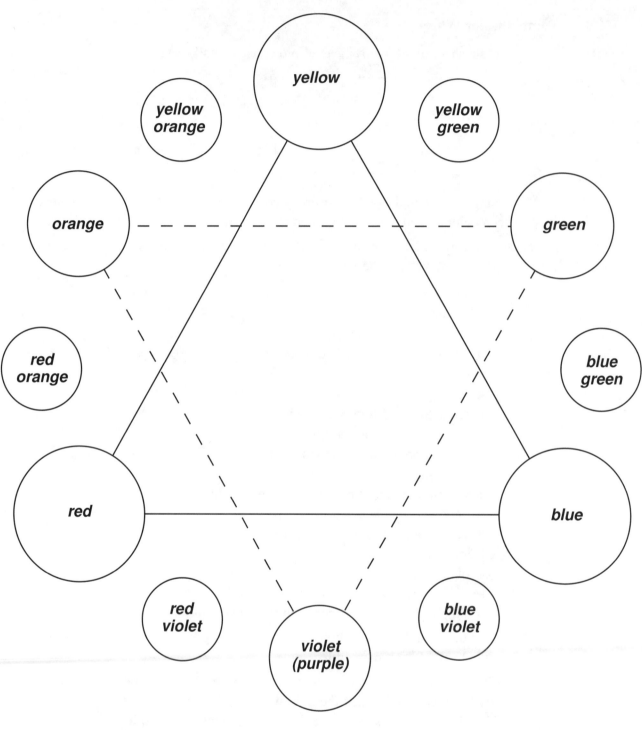

Primary Colors: ___***red, yellow, blue***___

Secondary Colors: ___***orange, green, violet***___

Complementary Colors: ___***colors directly across the color wheel from each other***___

THE COLOR WHEEL

Name: _____

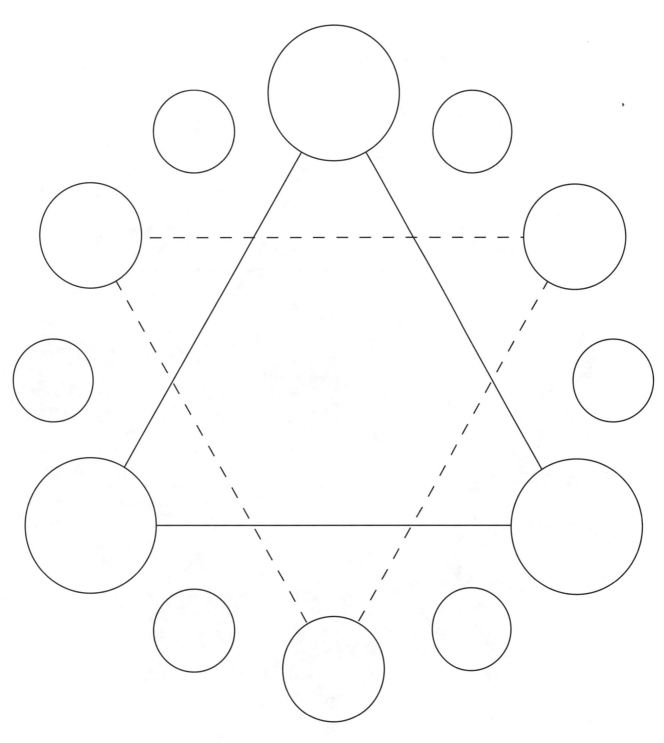

Primary Colors: _____

Secondary Colors: _____

Complementary Colors: _____

162

FROM LIGHT TO DARK

Concepts: Value scale from light to dark for one color; monochromatic color scheme

Skills: Planning; painting; mixing paint to create values

▶ ## Suggested Materials

- 12" × 18" white paper
- Tempera paint—black, white, and one other color
- Brushes
- Containers of water
- Pencils

▶ ## Directions

Value Scale (may be done as a teacher demonstration)

1. Fold a piece of paper into sixteen small rectangles.

2. Starting with white paint, add a small drop of the single color; paint the first rectangle. Continue this process for seven more rectangles, gradually adding more of the single color to make each rectangle progressively darker.

3. Clean your brush; paint the ninth space with just the single color (no black or white mixed in).

4. For the remaining seven spaces, gradually add a small drop of black to the single color to get progressively darker spaces. Caution: Adding black makes colors darken very fast.

Monochromatic Painting

1. Sketch a picture or a design on paper with a pencil. The picture or design should consist of enclosed spaces, not unattached lines.

2. Paint the picture using a monochromatic color scheme (the values from light to dark of only one chosen color). Mix the color with either black or white as desired. All three (black, white, and the color) should never be mixed together for this project since that would change the intensity (purity) of the color as well as its value.

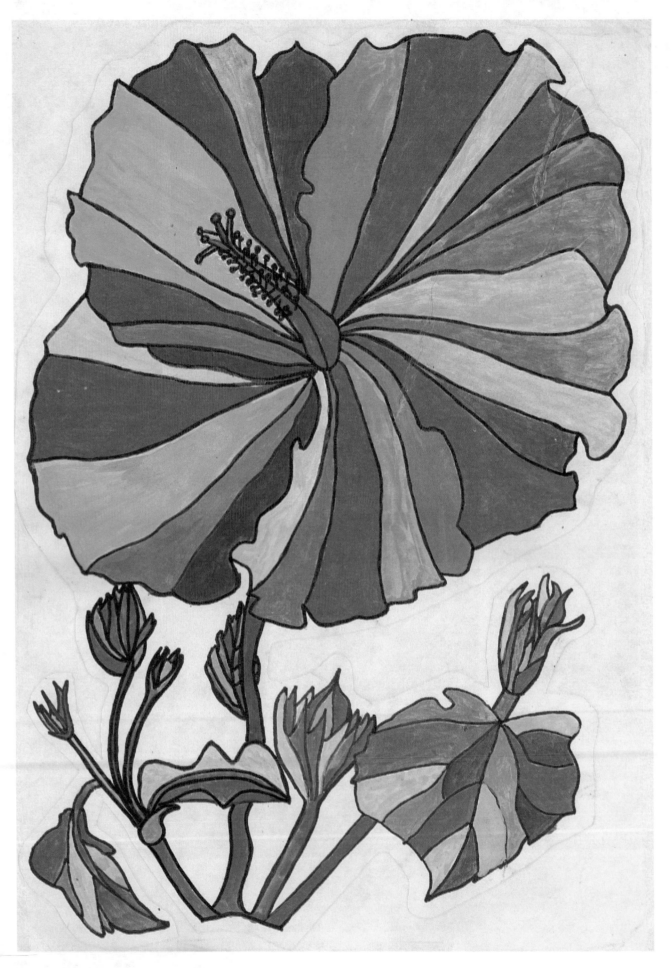

Tempera

COLOR MIX CARTOONS

Concepts: Mixing the primary colors to form other colors; distortion for comic effect

Skills: Drawing cartoon characters; painting; color mixing

▶ Suggested Materials

- Examples of a variety of simple cartoon characters
- 12" × 18" white paper
- Pencils
- Tempera paint—red, yellow, and blue
- Brushes
- Containers of water
- Permanent black markers (optional)

▶ Directions

1. Discuss and look at a variety of simple cartoon characters. Note that expressions, poses, and proportions are exaggerated and distorted for comic effect.

2. Sketch an original cartoon-style character on the 12" × 18" paper. Trace over the lines with a black marker if desired.

3. Using a brush and tempera paint, mix the primary colors (red, yellow, and blue) to achieve desired colors and paint the cartoon.

Note 1: If students have already done Lesson 47 (Color Wheel), they will know which colors to mix to create other colors. If not, give a brief demonstration and then encourage exploratory mixing as they work.

Note 2: For additional color-mixing experience, another picture could be done with black and white added to the primary color palette. This is particularly helpful if students have already completed Lesson 48 and learned about mixing values of a color.

WANT-AD BUILDINGS

▶ Suggested Materials

- Newspaper want ads
- Pencils
- Rulers
- Tempera paint
- Brushes
- Containers of water

▶ Directions

1. Choose a section of a want-ad page to use for your painting.

2. Draw one or several homes or buildings on the want-ad page; use the type and the lines dividing columns and ads as guidelines for drawing and painting.

3. Paint with tempera paint; add trees, flowers, cars, sidewalks, and so forth.

4. The background may be painted or left with the ads showing.

Concepts: Flexible and creative use of materials and techniques; knowledge about buildings and landscapes

Skills: Drawing; painting

Tempera

LESSON 51

SPONGE TREES

▶ Suggested Materials

- Trees or photographs of trees
- 9" × 12" paper
- Tempera paint
- Brushes
- Containers of water
- 1" sponge cubes
  (A dry, hard cellulose sponge can be cut into cubes with a sharp knife.)

▶ Directions

1. Observe trees or photographs of trees.

2. On 9" × 12" paper, decide where ground will be. Starting brush strokes at ground and brushing upward to branch tips, paint tree trunk and branches with brown paint. If desired, add strokes of black or white.

3. Paint a limited area of ground or grass surrounding the base of the trunk if desired.

4. Daub dry sponge cubes into paint and daub gently on the tree. Leave some open spaces.

5. Paint colors could be
   - Spring—pink, white, lavender, pale yellow, pale green
   - Summer—pink, yellow, different shades of green, purple
   - Fall—red, orange, yellow, brown
   - Winter—white, gray, brown, dull dark green for evergreen trees

Concepts: Knowledge of tree structure, shapes, and growth patterns; flexible use of materials and techniques

Skills: Using a sponge as a painting tool; painting trees

SCRAPE DESIGNS

▶ Suggested Materials

- White drawing paper
- Crayons
- Black tempera paint
- Sponge brushes
- Cardboard scrapers (approximately 1" × 3")

▶ Directions

1. Color heavily with wax crayons (one color or several) to fill the entire sheet of paper. Leave no uncolored areas.

2. Use a sponge brush to cover the entire paper quickly with black paint.

3. Immediately (while the paint is still wet) use cardboard scrapers to scrape off the paint in desired designs.

Concepts: Unity through common color; artistic uses of sponge brushes and cardboard

Skills: Using scraping technique to create color areas

FOAM TRAY OR PARAFFIN PRINTS

▶ Suggested Materials

- Foam meat trays or paraffin wax blocks
- Scissors
- Paper
- Pencils
- Tempera paint (plus several drops of detergent) or block printing ink (in tubes; water soluble)
- Brayer or paper towel inking pad
- Newspapers

▶ Directions

1. If using foam meat trays, cut off the turned-up edges.
2. On paper, sketch a design or picture the same size as your foam tray or paraffin block.
3. Transfer your design by placing it on top of the foam tray or paraffin block and tracing it with a dull pencil, pressing heavily to make deep grooves.
4. Apply ink or paint to the block, using a brayer if available.
5. If a brayer is not available, use tempera and press the design side of the block firmly down on a paint-coated "inking pad" of layers of damp paper towels. Lift off.
6. Place the block design-side down on paper lying on a newspaper cushion.
7. Press the block hard all over.
8. Lift the block; allow the print to dry.

Note: The printmaking process produces a reversed image. If letters, words, or numbers form part of the design, they must be put on the block in reversed form to be correct on the print.

Concepts: Knowledge of the printmaking process and how it can give multiple reversed images of the print block

Skills: Printmaking

CARDBOARD PRINTS

▶ **Suggested Materials**

- Paper
- Thin white cardboard
- Scissors
- White glue
- Tempera paint (plus several drops of detergent) or block printing ink (in tubes; water soluble)
- Brayer or paper towel inking pad
- Newspapers

▶ **Directions**

1. Plan a design on paper if desired.
2. Cut parts of the planned design out of cardboard.
3. Glue cardboard parts of the design onto a piece of cardboard backing to form your printing block. Start with the largest pieces, layering others.
4. Add glue dribbles and lines for more detail.
5. Let the glue dry thoroughly.
6. Apply ink or paint to the design, using a brayer if available.
7. If a brayer is not available, use tempera and press the design side of the block firmly down on a paint-coated "inking pad" of layers of damp paper towels. Lift off.
8. Place the block design-side down on paper lying on a newspaper cushion.
9. Press the block hard all over.
10. Lift the block; allow the print to dry.

Note: The printmaking process produces a reversed image. If letters, words, or numbers form part of the design, they must be put on the block in reversed form to be correct on the print.

Concepts: Knowledge of the relief printmaking process and how it can give multiple reversed images of the print block

Skills: Cutting; gluing; printmaking

Tempera

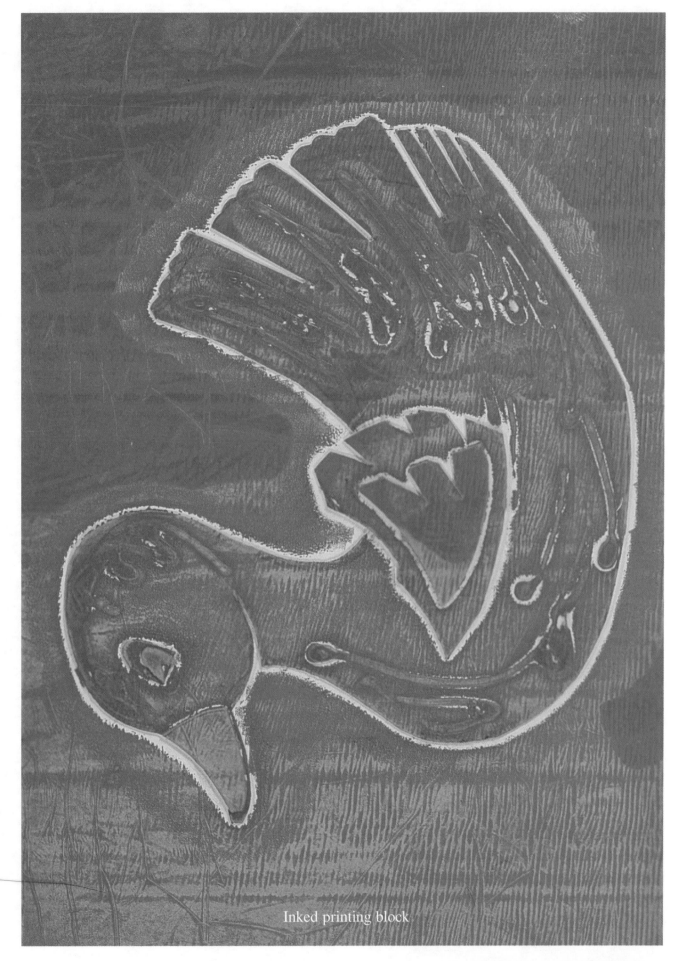

Inked printing block

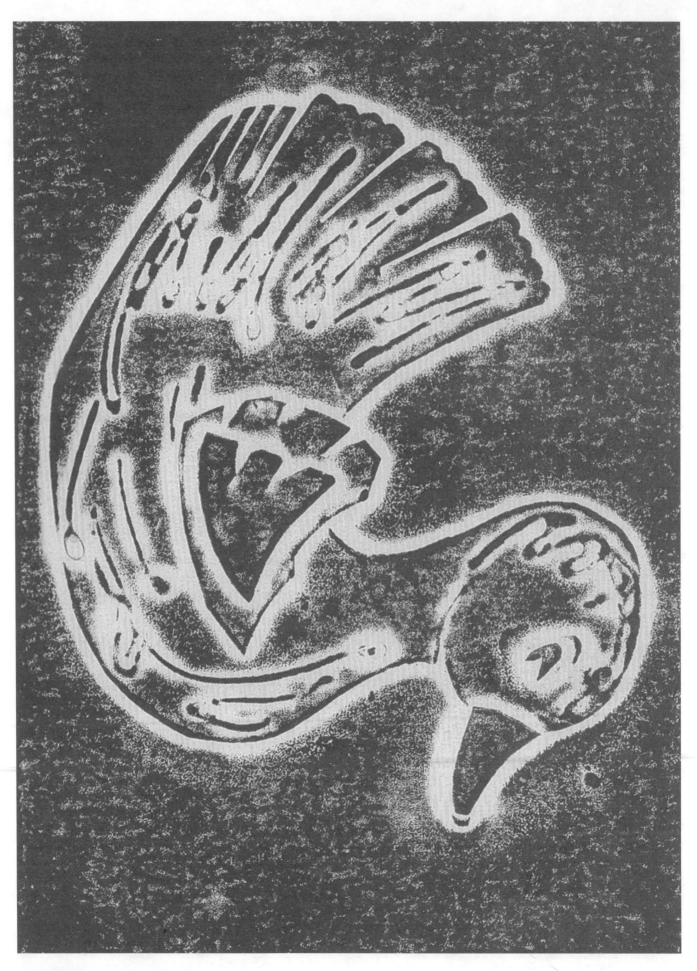

Tempera

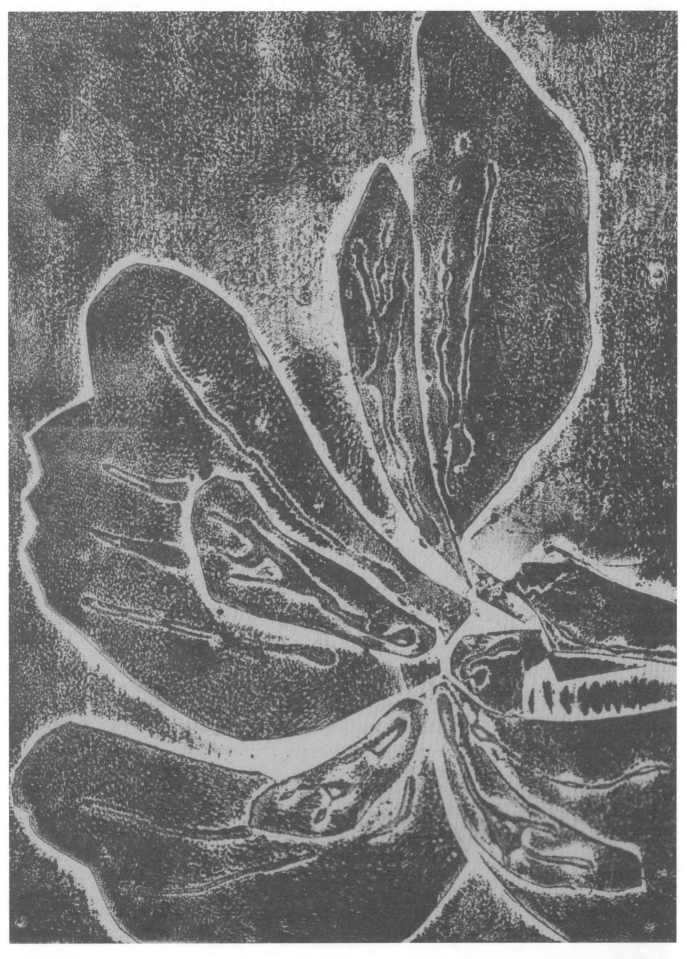

WATERCOLOR

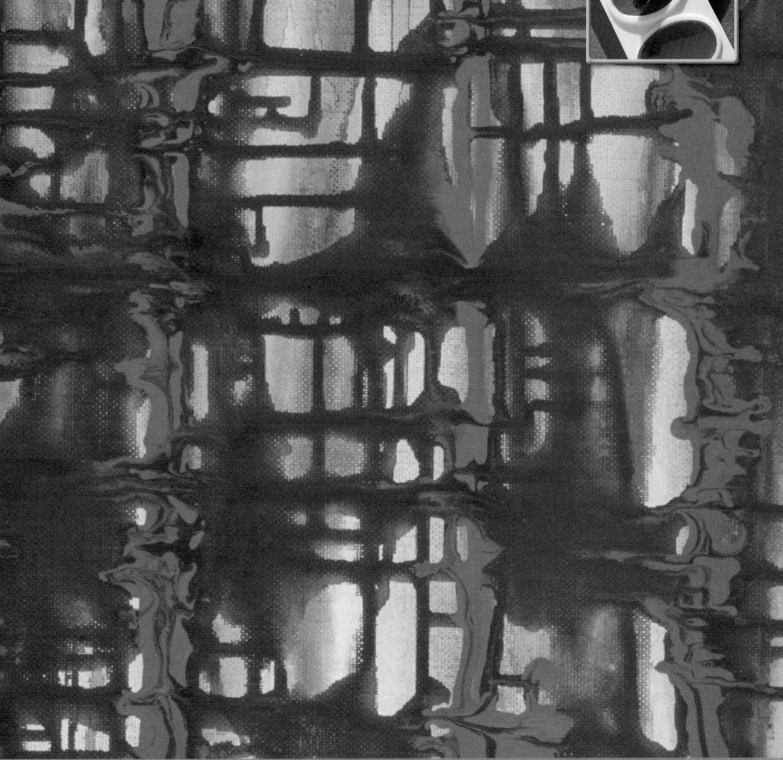

WATERCOLOR LANDSCAPES

Concepts: Atmospheric perspective (items farther away look paler and less detailed); wet, flowing characteristics of watercolor; effect of adding water to the colors; background, middleground, and foreground

Skills: Drawing; painting; creating appearance of atmospheric perspective

▶ Suggested Materials

- Landscapes or good photographs of landscapes
- 12" × 18" white paper (80 lb. drawing paper or heavier watercolor paper if available)
- Pencils
- Watercolors
- Brushes
- Containers of water

▶ Directions

1. Decide what type of landscape to paint and what to include in it.
2. Lightly sketch your idea onto the paper.
3. Paint the background (sky, mountains, etc.) first; use watery, pale colors.
4. Paint the middleground and foreground (grass, dirt, foliage, water, buildings, etc.) with stronger colors.
5. Allow to dry.
6. Continue painting more detailed parts of the picture, using soft, wet paint and very little additional water.

WATERCOLOR FLOWERS

Concepts: Characteristics of watercolor; knowledge of flower parts, shapes, and colors

Skills: Painting; using different brushstrokes

► Suggested Materials

- Flowers or good photographs of flowers
- Paper (80 lb. drawing paper or heavier watercolor paper if available)
- Pencils
- Watercolors
- Brushes
- Containers of water

Option: Use colored paper and use some white tempera paint for highlights (see page 192).

► Directions

1. Decide what type of flowers to paint.
2. Lightly sketch your idea onto the paper.
3. Paint the background (if any) first; use watery colors.
4. Allow to dry.
5. Continue painting more detailed parts of the picture, using soft, wet paint and very little additional water.
6. Use different types of brushstrokes to make petals, leaves, stamens, grass, vase, and so forth.

LEAF PRINTS

► Suggested Materials

- Watercolors
- Brushes
- Leaves (especially good are those with thick veins, such as geraniums)
- White, buff, or ivory paper
- Containers of water

► Directions

1. Paint watercolor directly on a leaf.

2. Press the leaf onto the paper; lift off.

3. Repeat. Leaf prints may touch or overlap.

Concepts: Pattern; transparent brilliance of watercolor; knowledge of leaf shapes and vein patterns; flexible and creative use of materials and techniques

Skills: Painting; printmaking

SILHOUETTES

▶ Suggested Materials

- 9" × 12" white paper
- 9" × 12" black paper
- Watercolors
- Brushes
- Pencils
- Rulers
- Scissors
- Glue
- Containers of water

▶ Directions

1. Wet white paper under the faucet or immerse in a pan or a sink.
2. Lay the wet paper flat on a desk or tabletop.
3. Paint stripes using bright colors, letting the colors run together. Allow to dry.
4. Draw a 1" border around the black paper.
5. Draw a picture in the center of the black paper. The picture should touch the border in at least two places.
6. Cut away background spaces.
7. Glue the black silhouette on the watercolor wash.

Note: Younger students with less skill handling scissors may draw a straight or curved horizon line on the black paper and make a silhouette attached to and above that line, with sides and top unbordered.

Concepts: Transparent color-blending qualities of watercolor; characteristics of silhouettes

Skills: Color blending; drawing; cutting; gluing

LESSON 59

WATERCOLOR STILL LIFE

Concepts: Balance; unity; proportion; still-life arrangement; characteristics of watercolor

Skills: Drawing; painting; using shading, color strength, and overlapping to create the illusion of three dimensions in watercolor

▶ Suggested Materials

- Objects to set up in a still-life arrangement (These should be fairly simple in design. Select objects that will work well together in color and size.)
- Cardboard boxes and scissors to use in making shadow boxes (optional)
- Large sheets of 80 lb. white drawing paper or heavier watercolor paper
- Pencils
- Watercolors
- Brushes
- Containers of water
- Scrap paper

▶ Directions

1. Arrange approximately five interesting objects so that they overlap somewhat and can be viewed as a unified group. Use a place mat or fabric beneath or behind objects. You might want to place the objects in a shadow box. (A shadow box can be made by cutting away three sides of a cardboard box and leaving two adjacent vertical sides and a bottom base.)
2. Sketch the objects, watching placement, relationship to one another, and shadows. Try to show a pleasing, harmonious view.
3. Paint the background first: use a thin wash of color and leave object areas unpainted. Using a complementary color (see Lesson 47) of the predominant color of the display is usually a good choice. Paint any shadows you see.
4. When the background is dry, begin painting the objects, using water sparingly so the colors will remain strong and bright.
5. To make objects appear round and to show their shadowed side, leave highlights white or paint a light color. Paint the shadows using a second layer of the same color, a darker related color, or a mixture of the color and a very small amount of the complementary color. Test on scrap paper to decide which you prefer.

ABSTRACT STILL LIFE

Concepts: Overlapping; abstraction (expressing the essence of the subject); symmetry

Skills: Drawing; cutting; painting; using markers

▶ ## Suggested Materials

- Scrap paper
- Scissors
- 12" × 18" white paper
- Pencils
- Wide-tip black markers (waterproof)
- Watercolors
- Brushes
- Containers of water

▶ ## Directions

1. Fold pieces of scrap paper in half.

2. Cut five to ten symmetrical objects (vases, cups, bowls, glasses, pots) from different pieces of scrap paper. Use the fold as the center line of each object. The objects should be a variety of sizes and shapes. For more variety cut one or two objects, such as cups or pitchers, that are not symmetrical.

3. Scatter and overlap the objects on 12" × 18" paper.

4. Choose one of the following styles and trace around the objects according to your chosen style:

   - Opaque objects—objects are partially hidden behind others (page 205). Leave off or erase parts of lines that would be behind other objects.
   - Transparent objects—every object is completely visible. Objects can be seen through the others (page 206).
   - Large section pieces—every object is completely visible and the entire paper is divided in several places with wide, straight lines (page 207). This style could also be used with other subjects for a stained glass window effect.

5. After drawing with the style you chose, outline accordingly with broad lines by using a black marker.

6. Paint the background and each section inside the black lines with watercolors. Switch colors each time you reach a black marker line.

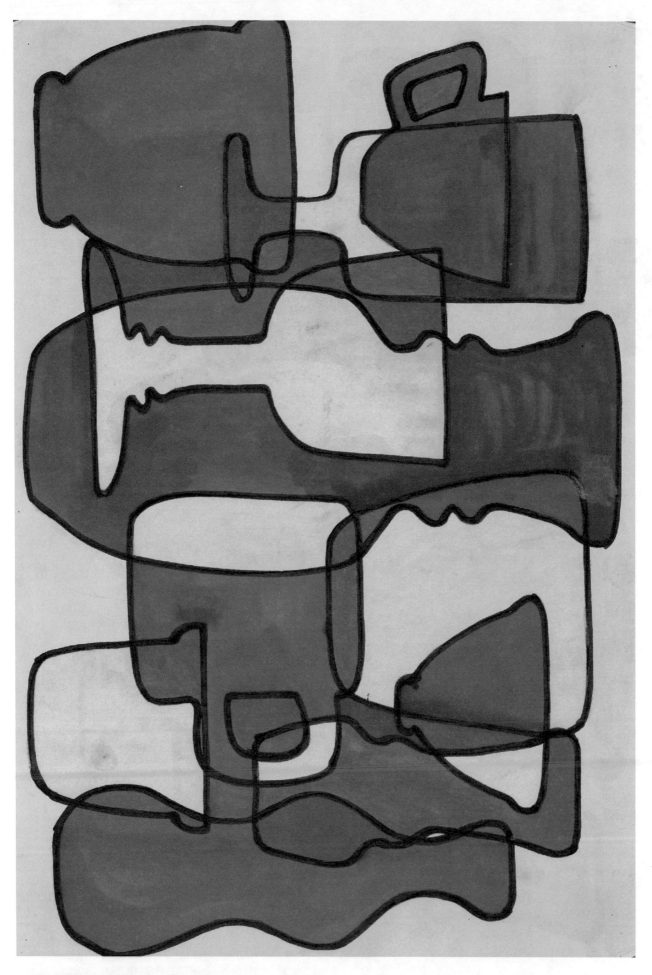

Watercolor

NOTES

Working Together

Whether you have been teaching for many years or are just getting started, your comments are vital in helping us maintain our standard of excellence. In fact, most of the improvements in our materials started with good advice from consumers. So after you have put our products to the test, please give us your thoughtful comments and honest assessment.

And thanks for your valuable help!

Book Title _____ Grade level _____

Material was ☐ used in classroom. ☐ used in home school. ☐ examined only.

How did you hear about us?
_____
_____
_____

I liked
_____
_____
_____

I'd like it better if
_____
_____
_____

How did our material compare with other publishers' materials?
_____
_____
_____

Other comments?
_____
_____
_____

(OPTIONAL)
☐ Dr. ☐ Miss ☐ Mrs. ☐ Mr. _____

School_____

Street_____

City_____State_____ZIP_____

Fold and tape. DO NOT STAPLE.
Mailing address on the other side.

BJU PRESS
Greenville, SC 29614

Phone(___)_____

E-mail _____

TAPE SHUT—DO NOT STAPLE

NO POSTAGE
NECESSARY IF
MAILED IN THE
UNITED STATES

BUSINESS REPLY MAIL

FIRST-CLASS MAIL   PERMIT NO. 344   GREENVILLE, SC

POSTAGE WILL BE PAID BY ADDRESSEE

BJU PRESS
TEXTBOOK DIVISION
1700 WADE HAMPTON BLVD.
GREENVILLE, SC 29609-9971

- - - - Fold here -

- - - - Fold here -